Magic
with
Everyday
Objects

GEORGE SCHINDLER

Magic with Everyday Objects

Over 150 tricks anyone can do at the dinner table

ILLUSTRATIONS BY ED TRICOMI

STEIN AND DAY/*Publishers*/New York

First published in 1976
Copyright © 1976 by George Schindler
All rights reserved
Designed by Ed Kaplin
Printed in the United States of America
Stein and Day/*Publishers*/Scarborough House, Briarcliff Manor, N.Y. 10510

Library of Congress Cataloging in Publication Data

Schindler, George.
    Magic with everyday objects

    Bibliography: p. 237
    Includes index.
    SUMMARY: Directions for performing approximately
100 magic tricks without sleight of hand, using everyday objects.
    1. Conjuring.   2.   Tricks.   [1.   Magic tricks]
I.   Title.
GV1547.S244   793.8   75–34265
ISBN 0–8128–1897–0

For Nina, Shari, Scott, and Dee,
who sat through every one of
these miracles.

ACKNOWLEDGMENTS

This work resulted indirectly from my association with the School for Magicians in New York City and the encouragement given me by my three partners: Frank Garcia, the most knowledgeable magician I know; Arnold Freed, a magician who creates laughter as an artist creates a painting; and Fred Ponger, a fine actor and level-headed businessman.

A final acknowledgment goes to Bob Reiss, a former student at our school. Bob's foresight in the field of "everyman's magic" has made magic widely available. His excellent *Magic Acts* may provide us with the magicians of tomorrow.

Contents

Introduction

This is a book for everybody who enjoys magic. It is not intended to make you a professional magician, but it will show you how to perform entertaining miracles that require no special skills or lengthy practice sessions. Whether you are a newcomer to the field or an old pro, the idea is to have fun.

Age is not a factor in using this book. If you are a student, a businessman or -woman, a retired grandparent, or just a person who loves fun, you will find these tricks easy to learn. You will spend little, if any, money on props, because the magic presented here is performed with the everyday objects found at any dinner table or in your pocket.

Magic has fascinated people for more than five thousand years. In ancient times it was closely associated with religion. A soothsayer, or magician, warned Caesar against the Ides of March. Shakespeare tells us that Macbeth conjured up visions. The wizard Merlin supposedly moved the giant stones to Stonehenge by causing them to fly through the air.

We are now living in the magical twentieth century, when visions travel through the air to our TV sets. Yet most people are still amazed at the same tricks our ancestors saw. Modern magicians in casual dress use techniques passed from one conjuror to the other for thousands of years.

Modern magic fools the mind as well as the eye, as you

will soon see. But before you attempt to digest this book in its entirety, scan it to get a feeling for the material. Read a trick or two from each of the four sections. The first section covers the magic done with props found on the table such as silverware, rolls and bread, napkins, dinnerware, salt and pepper. Read each trick with the props at hand so that you can follow the steps as you read. By the time you reach the conclusion of the description, you will have performed the trick. Ed Tricomi's illustrations should make every move clear and easy to follow. Now practice the trick a few times by yourself—in front of a mirror, if possible. Once you feel confident about the steps, do the trick for a member of your own family. Your family will be the hardest to fool. Once you have mastered the trick, present it to your friends at the next dinner party. Never do the same trick twice for the same audience.

The second section covers mentalism and ESP. This is a different kind of magic and should be performed a bit more seriously. Read the introduction for tips on how to present the tricks in this section. You will find that these experiments are not confined to the dinner table, but may also be used in the living room or for stage or platform performances. Some have been done on TV, a few even over the phone. Read these, too, with the props at hand, and work with someone in your family before you face an easier audience.

The third section of the book deals with tricks done using the props in your pocket—money, cigarettes, rubber bands, matches, etc. (Tricks using cigarettes and matches are not recommended for young performers.) Using a variety of props will add flexibility to your magic technique. You will find that other articles may be substituted for the ones we describe here, and that soon you can earn the reputation of being a magician by performing anywhere at any time with any props available.

The last part of this book, "Let Us Entertain Them," is the most important one. It explains how to make magic into the art form it is, how to combine tricks into an effective routine, and above all how to present yourself. Misdirection is probably the most valuable technique you can develop. Reread this section often as a reminder of how and why you are creating magic.

Whether you are a beginner or a polished performer, I hope you will not stop with this book. The material has been carefully selected from hundreds of magic secrets, some published and some unpublished. I have tried to cull the best available material in the category of tricks that require no special skills and use ordinary props. Many of the older tricks are new in modern dress. I did not invent these tricks, but I do claim originality in their presentation, derived from my thirty-four years' experience as a professional performer. The magic presented here has been developed by numerous members of the magic fraternity, whose devotion to magic is responsible for the advancement and continuity of the art. It is my hope that you join this fraternity and go on to the more advanced phases of magical entertainment. Whether you perform for money or as a hobby, you will bring happiness to your audience.

1

On the Table

Magic with Silverware

SWALLOWING THE SPOON

You have practiced this trick until you have it down pat, and now you are seated at the dinner table, waiting to find the right moment to amuse and puzzle your friends. You can't very well announce, *"Now I'm going to do a trick"*—you must be a bit more subtle.

Start with a casual remark: *"Isn't this an interesting spoon?"* Lift your teaspoon, rub the handle with the fingers of the other hand, and set the spoon on the table in front of you. The spoon should be parallel to the edge of the table, about three inches away from the edge. *"Did you ever notice the coating they put on spoons?"*

Hold the spoon as shown in Figure 1. The handle rests along the middle finger of your right hand. The bowl part sits in the left hand. The left middle finger and thumb hold it in place. The right thumb holds the handle in place. Both hands are together. Your thumbs are facing you; your fingers face the audience. Your right hand overlaps the left a bit so that

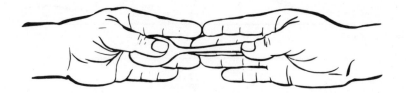

Figure 1

the index and ring fingers are almost touching. The spoon is completely hidden from view.

Raise the spoon, turning your left hand so that the spoon is in a vertical position as you bring both hands up to your mouth. Open your mouth as though you were a sword swallower ready to eat the spoon. Change your mind at the last moment, setting the spoon down on the table as it was before.

"We'll need a bit of seasoning." Pick up a salt or pepper shaker and sprinkle a bit on the spoon. Position your hands on the table in front of the spoon exactly as you did before (Figure 2). This time your thumbs do not hold on to the spoon. You slide the spoon toward your body. The hands come back to the edge of the table, where the spoon will drop into your lap. At this point be careful not to look down or even change your expression. Keeping your hands in the same position, lift them to your mouth, with the left hand vertical. There is actually nothing in the hands, but your moves will be the same as before.

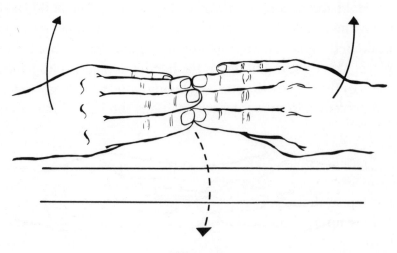

Figure 2

Pretend to insert the spoon into your mouth and begin to chew as your hands come away from your mouth. Your tongue in your cheek will help the illusion a bit. Pretend to push the spoon a bit more into your mouth with one finger. Swallow very hard as if it were a chore. A sip of water here might be convincing. *"You know, that wasn't as good as I thought it would be. They just don't make spoons the way they used to."*

After the trick is over, you can drop one hand into the lap and quietly slip the spoon onto the table when the next course is served, or at a moment when no attention is on you. If you are going to do other tricks just leave it in your lap. You might work it into your sleeve and later in the meal pull it out, remarking, *"Gee, I almost forgot to return this."* This brings a laugh, and your spectators will give you credit for great sleight-of-hand ability.

As with other tricks you will find in this book, you need not use a spoon. You can "swallow" a knife, pencil, or any long flat object that will fit in your palms.

CHEAP SILVER

Your hostess at dinner might be most apprehensive about this next miracle. The first step is to procure a nickel or a dime, which will secretly be held between your thumb and the first joint of your right index finger. If a nickel or dime is not available, any silver coin will do. Your hand can rest in your lap so that the coin is not seen.

Pick up a teaspoon with your left hand. Look at it very closely as if studying the pattern. *"What kind of metal is this?"* If it is silver the hostess will proudly tell you, but no matter what she replies you will say, *"It must be that new flexible alloy."*

Hold the spoon vertically so that the bowl touches the table. You now bring up the right hand, pressing the coin against the top of the spoon handle. Your middle and ring finger wrap around the handle; the pinky slips *behind* it. The left hand curls around the bottom fingers of the right hand so that only the bowl of the spoon is now seen on the tabletop. The edge of the coin will appear to be the top of the spoon handle (Figure 3).

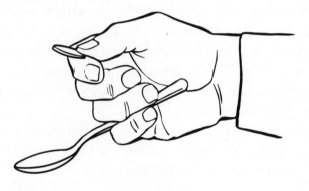

Figure 3

"Look how soft this is." Move the right hand forward, bending it at the wrist. The spoon will rest at a forty-five-degree angle on the pinky. The left hand covers the action by applying a bit of pressure toward your body. The illusion is perfect. The spoon will appear to have been bent in half. Before the hostess screams, pull the spoon away from the table with the left hand. The right hand drops back into your lap with its coin. Drop the spoon with a clang. *"Don't worry, it straightens itself out when it hits the table."*

SNAP VANISH

After a few good tricks you are bound to be invited out to dinner again. Naturally you are not going to do the same tricks. Never repeat any trick, no matter how much your audience pleads, unless it is designed to be repeated as part of the routine.

Here is a variation of the Swallowing the Spoon effect. In the last version you used the misdirection of putting the spoon back on the table before the final vanish. In this case you will also use your eyes to divert the spectator. This is best done when seated directly opposite your victim.

Pick up a teaspoon and wave it back and forth a bit to establish that it is really there. Set it on the table and conceal it with your hands exactly as you did for the Swallowing trick. Now look the spectator straight in the eye as you pull the spoon back and drop it into your lap. *"Keep your eyes on the spoon"*—you will say this after the spoon has gone.

Then thrust both hands toward the spectator and snap them as if breaking the spoon in half. At the same time, make a clicking noise by snapping your tongue against your upper palate. Both the click and the hand movement will startle the spectator for a second. Open your hands and show that the spoon has vanished. *"It's gone! You didn't watch me carefully enough."*

TRANSFORMATION

A transformation effect—changing one object into another—will always create the element of surprise, which is

very important in performing magic. This trick requires a
large cloth napkin, a knife, and a spoon. In order to make
room for the napkin you will have to move various objects
from the table. As you do so, you must secretly place the
knife in position so that when you spread the napkin
diagonally in front of you, the knife will be hidden beneath
it. You are now ready to begin.

Pick up a teaspoon and place it in the center of the
napkin next to the hidden knife (Figure 4).

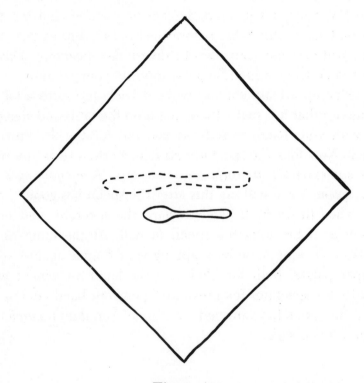

Figure 4

*"Science has never been able to explain this unusual
experiment."* Fold the bottom half of the napkin up and

away from you so that it rests about an inch from the top corner (Figure 5).

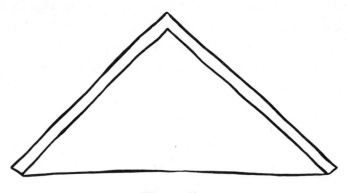

Figure 5

Both objects are now out of sight. Place your hands on the napkin so that your thumbs are under the spoon, fingers around the knife. Lift both slightly and begin to roll the napkin toward your body so that the knife and spoon are both rolling together. Two or three rolls will secure them in place (Figure 6).

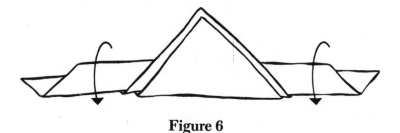

Figure 6

With the left hand, grab the napkin and utensils so that the thumb is under them and your fingers on top. Lift the parcel and turn it over. Your palm faces upward as you set it back on the table. Roll the napkin "away from" you this time. Continue to roll until you have both corners together, facing away from you. Slide the package so that it rests about two inches from the edge of the table. Your left thumb and forefinger take the bottom flap and hold it firmly. The right thumb and forefinger pull back the top flap so that you have the napkin as in Figure 7.

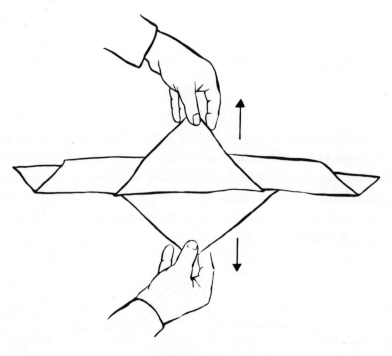

Figure 7

The right hand now pulls the top corner up and away from the table toward your body. The angle should be about forty-five degrees. If done correctly the napkin opens and exposes the knife. The spoon will drop into your lap. A snap of the wrist will cause the knife to drop with a loud clang.

As you are doing the rolling you can patter. *"If we wrap the spoon in the cloth it will become very warm. The heat building up inside causes a physical change known as the Clang Phenomenon."*

After the napkin is unrolled, with the resulting noise as the knife hits the table, you continue: *"Did you hear the clang?"* Pick up the knife, dip it in the butter dish, and proceed to butter a slice of bread casually. *"Just what I needed. A hot knife."*

FLYING SPOON

Levitation is the act of causing an object to rise and float in the air.

Levitation tricks are usually done in theaters where the stage can accommodate the necessary equipment, but this one can be done at dinner. Our object will be a spoon. To help with the illusion we will use the table magician's most useful servant, the lap.

Before introducing the effect, slip a spoon and a fork into your lap. Under the table you will attach the spoon to the fork so that the spoon handle is firmly wedged between the middle tines of the fork. When the fork is attached to the bottom of the spoon handle they will form a right angle. This arrangement is on your lap with the bowl of the spoon facing the spectator opposite you. Cover the two pieces with a napkin.

"I must tell you about a crazy dream I had last night. Can we clear the table a bit?" Clear the entire area in front of you on the table. Reach into your lap and pick up the napkin in the following manner: The right thumb and middle finger firmly grip the end of the fork handle under the napkin. The

right index finger grabs the outside of the napkin about an inch from the hem nearest your body. The left hand takes the left end of the napkin the same way on the other side.

Lift the napkin from your lap. The fork and spoon should be hidden from view as you quietly lay the entire works on the table in front of you. The napkin will appear to be flat on the table. The spoon will be resting under the center of the napkin with the bowl still pointing toward the spectator. *"I dreamed that I was in my living room one evening when I heard a scratching noise coming from under my rug. It looked as though some small creature was trying to get out."*

As you speak gently press the right finger downward, the thumb slightly upward. This will lift the spoon. Set it down again. Do this twice. *"Suddenly it started to move strangely and appeared to be levitating itself off the floor."* Lift the fork about five inches off the table—the shape of the spoon will be satisfactorily vague.

"It kept getting higher and higher." Lift the fork so that the napkin is completely off the table. Now bring both hands together slightly and pretend that the object is floating around the table. If you keep your hands the same distance apart while moving them over the table you will create a perfect floating illusion.

"Finally I saw what the creature looked like. He was all dressed in silver and had a head like a spoon." At this point bring the napkin closer to your body. Tilt the fork upward so that the bowl of the spoon is showing behind the cloth (Figure 8).

If you turn your right wrist sideways the spoon will float back toward you. Move it back and forth a few times, keeping the fork out of view. Make sure that there is no light coming from behind you. If there is any, keep the spoon in front of your body.

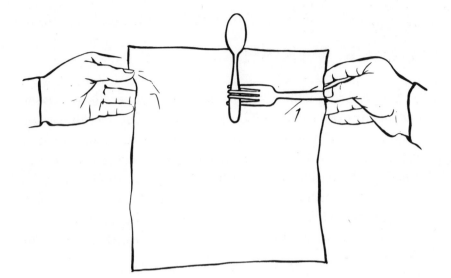

Figure 8

"It was spooky. I watched him fly around the room." Have the spoon go back under the cloth and by bringing the hands together and raising them, the entire thing appears to float upward.

Finally, lower the napkin so that the bottom edge is just below the table line. The left hand pulls at the top of the spoon, letting go of the napkin. The right hand drops into the lap, taking the fork away. Bring the right hand out again, leaving the fork in the lap, and reach for the top of the spoon. Bring both hands down to the table. *"When he got close enough I grabbed him to see who he was. He confessed and said he was a lost flying spoon. I asked, 'Where do flying spoons come from?' His answer was straight: 'From flying saucers.'"*

Hand the spoon to the spectator. *"Maybe it wasn't a dream after all!"*

QUICK VANISH

Here is a quickie that will require practice. Place a spoon perpendicular to the edge of the table. The handle should point toward you. The fingers of the right hand slightly overhang the end of the bowl. Tip the bowl slightly to lift the handle about half an inch, then with a quick backward movement brush the spoon into your right coat sleeve. When done very quickly this is a startling vanish. As soon as you feel the spoon in the sleeve, lift your hand to show your empty palm.

RUBBER KNIFE

You may remember this one from your childhood days. This is truly an optical illusion, where the eye plays tricks on the spectators. Hold a knife by its handle so that your thumb is underneath and the index finger on top. Do not hold it too tightly. Move the wrist up and down in an arc of about three or four inches. Because you are holding the knife off center it will wobble in a strange fashion, looking as though it were made of rubber.

"This must be a butter knife. It certainly doesn't look sturdy enough to cut bread."

MUSICAL KNIFE

With knife in hand you can now go into another stunt quite naturally. *"This is a very musical knife. It also has the same power as a divining rod. This knife can find water. I'll show you."*

Set three glasses in front of you. Put water in any one of them. The other two remain empty. Hold a silver fork firmly in your left hand, with the tines up. Your right hand holds the knife handle. Snap one of the tines of the fork so that it vibrates and hold the knife directly over an empty glass. *"Nothing here. No sound. No water."* Do the same with the second empty glass. *"No water here either."*

On the third try hold the knife over the glass containing the water. At the same time, touch the handle of the fork to the table. It will act as a tuning fork. The table acts as a sounding board, and you will get a high musical tone that seems, because of your misdirection, to come from the glass.

KNIFE SUSPENSION

While this falls into the category of magic, it is really a mysterious puzzle or table stunt. Call it a demonstration of magnetism. *"I am going to set up a magnetic field that is most unusual."* Pick up a knife and rub it on the tablecloth a few times. Now lay it on the table so that the handle extends over the edge on your side of the table. Drop your hands into your lap. *"I have just charged the knife with static electricity from the tablecloth."* In your lap you are positioning your fingers as shown in Figure 9.

Both palms are face up. Bend your ring fingers up and in toward the palms. The right pinky slides between the little finger and middle finger of the left hand, filling the space made by the bent ring fingers. The right middle finger is placed into the left hand between the left middle and index fingers. The right index finger slides on top of the left index

The hands are clasped into this position with fingers
ing one another on the back of the hands. This should
take a moment.

Your hands come from your lap and are positioned
directly under the extended knife handle. Bring your hands
up so that only the thumbs are at table height. The thumbs
grasp the knife at the point where the blade and handle
meet. The hands cup around the knife handle, which is now
pinched between the two ring fingers like a vise (Figure 10).
The palms come together and the knife is lifted. The handle
is hidden behind your hands, with the blade seen between
the thumbs. Bring your hands up in front of you so that the
audience sees the back of them.

"As I move my thumbs away from the blade I will blow
cool air to stimulate the molecules. Which is unusual, since I
have been using a lot of hot air up until now." Blow on the
blade and move your thumbs away from the knife. It will
appear to be suspended in air behind your hands. "As you
can see, the knife is losing its charge." Grab the blade with
your thumbs and separate your hands, allowing the knife to
drop onto the table. "This is a free trick—only the knife was
charged, not you."

Figure 9

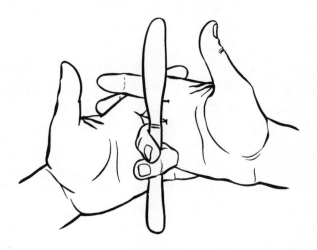

Figure 10

Salt, Pepper, and Sugar Necromancy

SALT GONE

Magicians from all over the world make it a point to stop at the Magicians' Table when visiting New York. Every weekday at lunchtime Rosoff's Restaurant sets aside a small area for the local magicians. Hobbyists and professionals meet there to chat, have lunch, and show one another the latest in magic miracles.

A newcomer is always treated to a performance by our dean, Joe Barnett, who is best known for his Salt Trick. Mr. Barnett causes a shaker full of salt to vanish before your eyes. Then he makes the salt reappear in a most comical manner.

We are going to do a simple version of the first half of this great stunt, which will not require sleight of hand. I urge you to read this explanation very carefully, since it uses the most basic of all magic concepts: misdirection. We will lead the spectator's attention away from what is actually happening.

Prepare for the trick by secretly slipping a paper napkin into your left coat pocket. Spread the napkin out so that it makes a lining for the pocket.

"Let me show you something unique that my doctor recommended." Pick up the salt shaker so that everyone can see the salt. Shake it back and forth a bit. Your left hand holds the shaker off the table close to your body. Slowly

unscrew the metal cap with your right hand. Your right hand now reaches across the table to the spectator farthest from you. Offer him the cap. *"I want you to hold on to this cap and make sure that I do not touch it at any time."* All the audience attention should now be on the cap.

Your left hand is busy in the meantime. You will dump all the salt from the shaker into the napkin in your left pocket. Bring your left hand back to the table, with all the fingers wrapped around the salt shaker so that no one can see inside. Open your right hand to show it empty. *"Watch."* Form a fist with your right hand, with an opening at the top where the index finger curls next to the thumb.

Pretend to pour the salt from the shaker into the opening. This is done by putting the top of the shaker on your right fist and merely turning the whole thing over with one move. Keep your right fist tightly closed as you openly place the empty salt shaker on the table. *"We will need the cap now."* Gesture to the spectator holding the cap. *"Please wave the cap over the top of the salt and watch what happens."*

After he has passed it over your hand, slowly open your fist, one finger at a time from the bottom up: pinky, ring finger, middle finger, index, and thumb in that order. *"The salt is gone!"* Screw the cap back on the shaker and set it in front of the spectator. *"Now you see why my doctor likes this trick. I'm on a salt-free diet."*

At the first opportunity, excuse yourself and head for the washroom to get rid of the napkin full of salt. Remove the napkin carefully, or you'll spend the rest of the month getting particles of salt from your pocket.

VANISHING SALT SHAKER

Misdirection is the magician's most valuable tool. The effect that you are now going to create is probably the best example of how misdirection works for the trickster. Every step in this trick is designed to lead the spectator astray. The final element of surprise will make this the most talked-about trick in your dinner table repertoire.

All that is required is a salt shaker and a paper napkin. The salt shaker should be within your reach but not prominent. Other dinner-table objects should remain on the table.

"I'd like to borrow a coin if I may. Actually, I'd like to borrow a hundred dollars, but for now a coin will do." Take a coin from one of your spectators. We will assume that it is a nickel. Drop the coin from a height of about six inches so that it hits the table and bounces. *"Can you see the coin from there? Is it heads or tails up?"*

Move the coin so that it rests about five inches from the edge of the table directly in front of you. Assuming the tail side is up, you say, *"This is the tail side. I'll show you the head side."* Turn the coin over. *"Now will you please verify this. Which side is up, heads or tails?"* He will answer, *"Heads."* *"Would you bet on it?"* At this point the spectator will of course make such a bet.

No matter what his answer you continue, *"Suppose I cover it up with something."* Look around the table for a suitable object. *"Let's use this salt shaker."* Cover the coin. *"Now, is the head side up or is the tail side up?"* Wait for an answer. *"Would you bet on it now?"* The spectator will now become a bit leery but will still bet heads. Lift the shaker straight up. *"You would have bet and won."*

Cover the coin with the shaker. This time pick up the paper napkin. *"Let's make it more difficult."* Open the napkin and place it on the salt shaker so that the center of the napkin is on top. Wrap the napkin loosely around the shaker so that it is completely covered. Do not wrap too tightly or the paper will tear. You should be able to lift the covered salt shaker and napkin with one hand. The right thumb and forefinger on the bottom of the shaker will do the lifting. Do not lift as yet.

"Now that I have covered the coin so you can't see it, is it heads or tails?" It makes no difference what he replies. Lift the napkin and shaker about an inch off the table. Bring your right hand back toward you, past the edge but level with the table. Use the index finger of your left hand to slide the coin away from you so that it will sit in the center of the table. As your audience is watching this move, relax pressure of your right thumb and the shaker will drop into your lap (Figure 11).

The napkin will still retain its shape, so be careful not to squeeze it as you bring it back to the center of the table to cover the coin.

"Heads or tails?"

He will answer, *"Heads."*

"What is heads? The coin? What coin? The nickel? What nickel? The one under the salt shaker? What salt shaker?" Saying this, slap your left hand onto the napkin and press it flat against the table. *"There is no shaker here!"*

You can use alternate endings for this trick. You can move the saltshaker off your lap and bring it under the table

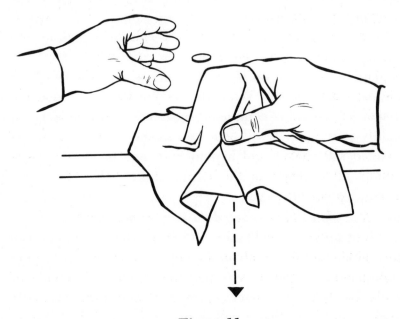

Figure 11

to a spot below the coin. Then announce, *"It went right through the table!"* Bring it out from under and set it on the table.

Another way to finish the trick would be to run the salt shaker up under your jacket, pretend to remove it from an inside pocket and place it on the table. The best thing to do is to leave it on your lap and later, at some opportune time, slip it back to the table.

Let's analyze the trick to see how misdirection works. The buildup at the beginning centered around the coin. Your spectator was watching the coin carefully, expecting you to do something that would cause the coin to flip over. The movement of the coin to the center of the table had all eyes following. This allowed you to drop the shaker into your lap unnoticed. The shape of the shaker under the napkin was also part of the misdirection. All the spectators would swear that they saw the shaker on the table before your hand came down on it.

This trick can be varied by using a stiff cloth napkin, which would also hold the shape. A newspaper wrapped properly would do just as well. Instead of a saltshaker you could use a small glass. Have the spectator hold his or her hand over the glass and startle him by pressing his own hand to the table to cause the vanish.

You will soon be aware of the importance of using your lap. Here are a few pointers to make that easier. Sit comfortably at the table with both feet on the floor and your knees together. You might place a handkerchief or napkin in your lap to catch the vanished objects. And a most important tip: *Never look down* when an object drops to your lap. Your eyes are very important in misdirection. If you look down, your spectator will do the same. If you look straight at him, his eyes will stay with yours.

SWEET AND GO

Now that you are an expert in the art of misdirection, you can vary your performances by doing this version of the previous trick. Vanishing the sugar substitute is another easy one covered by misdirection. This effect involves a packet of saccharin and a pepper shaker. You can see that it is easy to vary the objects used to do some of the same tricks. The pepper should be an arm's length away from you.

Take a package of saccharin from the sugar bowl. *"Did you know that saccharin causes strange reactions when combined with certain other chemicals?"* Bring the packet to a point on the table two inches directly in front of you. *"Saccharin reacts with pepper, for example."* As you speak, your right hand reaches across the table for the pepper shaker. Your left hand covers the saccharin packet and slides it toward the edge of the table, allowing it to drop to your lap. Close your left hand and bring it to the center of the table to meet the pepper. Both movements are done simultaneously. The move for the pepper shaker should get the attention away from the saccharin.

You now have a closed left fist in the center of the table. You are holding the pepper shaker so that all your fingers are wrapped around the glass. Your thumb covers the cap. Sprinkle a bit of pepper into your left fist. Bring the pepper back toward the edge of the table. At the same time lift your left fist for misdirection. The pepper will drop into your lap as you speak: *"Pepper causes the saccharin to disappear."* Bring your right hand back onto the table as though you were still holding the shaker. Open your left fist with a flourish. *"On the other hand, saccharin makes pepper vanish."* Open your right hand to show it empty. Do not attempt to retrieve either object.

RUN, PEPPER, RUN

With a little imagination you can make up your own patter or stories to go along with your magic. Patter is often the key to making a trick interesting. You must avoid boring your audience. The patter used in this book is generally very simple and should be used only as a guide—change it to fit your own style and personality.

The patter used for this particular miracle will appeal to

children as well as adults. At the end of the explanation you will see how to change the theme, using the same steps with different patter.

Find an excuse to leave the table. Go into the kitchen or the washroom and rub a generous amount of wet soap or liquid detergent onto the tip of your index finger. Come back to the table and start right off with your story.

"I just saw a crazy thing outside. Do you know that bank down the street?" (Don't worry if there isn't a bank down the street—if anyone calls that to your attention you remark, *"That's what makes this crazy."*) *"Let me show you what I saw."* Pour some water into a deep dessert dish or an empty ashtray. *"This is the bank. The water in it is for people who want to float loans. [Pause.] I'm sorry about the joke; let me go on with my story. There were a lot of people working in the bank."* Sprinkle a liberal amount of salt into the water. *"These are the people."* Stir the salt a bit with the index finger of the other hand, the one *without* the soap.

"Suddenly a bunch of men dressed in black ran into the bank. They all had guns and wore black masks." Pick up the pepper shaker and sprinkle pepper into the water to represent the men. *"They were just about to rob the bank when a brave teller sounded the alarm and walked right into the center of the bank."* Raise your soaped index finger and gently dip it into the water. The soap will form an invisible film on the surface of the water and the pepper will appear to run to the far sides of the dish. *"They all ran away, leaving the money behind. They got out into the street, where they were caught by the police. Now the only reason I can see for your not believing my story is that it's a lie."*

Your spectators will try the trick and of course will be unsuccessful without the small dab of soap. If you are doing this at home you can take the dish to the sink and fill it with water. This will give you a perfect chance to get to the detergent. Make sure that your finger is still soapy before you begin.

Here is another patter theme you might like. You explain that you live in a neighborhood with a community swimming pool. The dish represents the pool. *"Lots of people swim there."* Sprinkle the salt. *"Women"*—sprinkle some pepper—*"and men. One day a magician came to the pool and offered to show them a few coin tricks."* Dip your finger into the water. Look a bit surprised to see the pepper running away. *"They obviously didn't like coin tricks. Gee, I hope you don't feel the same way. I have a few great coin tricks I'd like to show you."*

Do another trick while you have the opening.

MYSTIC SHAKER

The recent renaissance of magic has brought ancient illusions to the attention of modern audiences. Many people have heard about these illusions but have never seen them. One such illusion is "levitation," which defies the laws of gravity. Perhaps you may have seen the Floating Lady on TV. A girl, covered only by a thin cloth, mysteriously rises up from a table. As she floats into the air the magician pulls the sheet away, and she is gone! There are many variations of the levitation effect: magicians levitate their assistants on flying carpets, on broomsticks, and into thin air.

At the dinner table the magician is limited in his scope but nevertheless can perform a levitation illusion.

You are going to use a toothpick, which must never be seen by your audience. (Any unseen tool used by the magician to accomplish his trick is called a gimmick.) The gimmick is held in your right hand. It rests behind the middle finger pointing downward toward the fingernail and is held in place by your thumb. A salt shaker is nearby.

"For centuries ancient and modern magicians have been performing illusions that defy all known laws of science. Their secrets have been passed from generation to generation. From my great-grandfather I learned to master the difficult technique of levitation."

As you speak you must bring the salt shaker to a position about eight inches in front of you on the table. Your thumb and middle finger press the toothpick into one of the center holes on top of the shaker so it is wedged firmly in the cap. The other fingers rest vertically on top of the shaker (Figure 12).

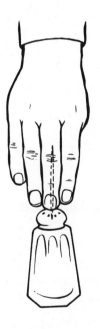

Figure 12

"Rise!" Command the salt shaker to action. Lift your arm straight up and off the table. Your right thumb is holding the toothpick against the middle finger. Bring the shaker to a position about three inches off the table. *"The salt shaker levitates without any visible means of support. Reminds me of my brother-in-law."* Curl the right pinky and ring fingers back. Point your index finger and raise the shaker a bit higher (Figure 13).

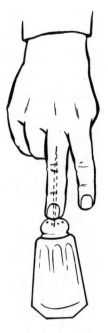

Figure 13

Bring the shaker back to the table gently and remove your right hand, making sure that you do not expose the gimmick. *"You have just witnessed a miracle!"*

OSMO-SALT

You are now in the process of learning many of the basic principles in the art of magic. Once you have learned them you will find that you can make up new tricks by interchanging the objects used. The principle you are about to learn can be used for a variety of other tricks, limited only by your own imagination.

You will need a table knife, which will be used for what professional magicians call the "paddle move." The trick also involves some salt and a napkin.

Ask your spectator to remove the cap from the salt shaker. While this is being done, secretly wet your index finger by dipping it into a glass of water. Touch the wet finger to one side of the blade of the knife to make an inconspicuous wet spot.

"Please pour a bit of salt into my palm and I'll show you an interesting phenomenon." Extend your open left hand. Pick up the knife with your right hand. The knife should be held so that your palm is up, with your right thumb holding the handle at the point where it meets the blade (Figure 14). The blade is pointing away from your body; the handle rests on the fingers of the open hand. The wet spot is on the upper surface of the blade. Do not call attention to it—the attention should be directed to the salt in the left palm. Pour the salt from the left hand onto the blade of the knife. Some of it will secretly stick to the wet spot. Shake the knife gently to allow the excess salt to fall off, while keeping the blade level so as not to tip off the fact that some of the salt is stuck there. *"This is all the salt we need."* Blow away the loose salt grains left in your open palm, and show that your left hand is now

empty. Bring the knife toward your left palm, and begin to close your left fingers over the knife blade. Roll the handle toward your body by exerting a little pressure with the right thumb. The edge of the knife is in the palm. It should look as if you were dumping the salt into your left hand. Close your left hand and draw the knife out. The position of the knife on your right hand should not change except that this time the clean side of the knife is facing upward.

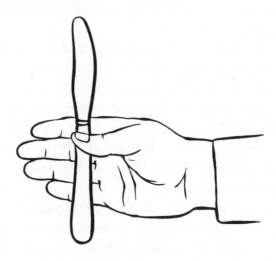

Figure 14

Use the knife to gesture toward your left palm. *"The salt is safe in here for a moment."* The knife is still held on the open palm as in Figure 14. You will now turn the palm downward by turning only your wrist, moving it toward your body. At the same time, the right thumb will roll the handle toward the finger tips. The knife will turn over but the movement of the wrist will mask the turn (Figure 15).

You have just created the effect that you have shown the opposite side of the knife, while in fact, you have shown the same side twice. By reversing the procedure you can show the knife in the first position again. Only the clean side is seen—the salt is hidden under the blade. Repeat the move.

Now place the point of the knife under a napkin so that you can lift the napkin slightly off the table, forming a tentlike shape. Slide the knife into the space between the napkin and the table while secretly turning the blade up. *"Watch how science and magic work together."* Hold the left hand over the top of the napkin. *"The salt will vanish and penetrate the napkin by invisible osmosis."* The left fingers point downward as you pretend to sprinkle the salt from the hand. Open your hand and show that the salt is gone. Slowly draw the knife from under the napkin, exposing the side with the spot of salt. Rub the salt off the blade and leave the knife on the table for examination.

The paddle move is relatively simple, but it can be made smoother if you are not self-conscious about turning the knife. Take special care not to use a very sharp knife so that you won't cut yourself—a butter knife will be effective.

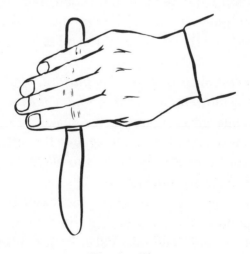

Figure 15

SODIUM CHLORIDE

Now that you are a master of the paddle move, you will be able to perform other miracles. Here is an impossible trick you can do. Secretly pour a small mound of salt on the tablecloth at your right next to a knife. A napkin is at your left, along with a salt shaker. Try not to set the objects in place in an obvious manner. Merely move them about on the table casually as if to make room for your miracle. Before you get ready to perform, secretly wet your left ring finger by dipping it into some water.

"A working knowledge of chemistry is a great help to a magician. Did you know that metals attract sodium chloride when combined with oxygen? You didn't know that? Let me demonstrate."

Pick up the knife at your right. *"This is a good metal to use."* Your left hand picks up the napkin and wipes the knife blade a few times. On the third wipe the left ring finger wets the underside of the blade as the napkin comes away from the knife.

"The metal must be free of impurities." Point to the salt shaker with your left hand. *"May I have the sodium chloride, please."* While all eyes are on the shaker, your right hand presses the wet side of the knife against the salt grains on the table. Some of the salt adheres to the blade. *"Common table salt, of course, is sodium chloride."*

Lift the knife from the table and casually turn it over using the paddle move. You are showing the same side twice, concealing the salt. The salt shaker is now taken with your left hand. A sudden upward movement of your arm will cause a few grains of salt to fly out through the holes in the cap. At the same time your right hand thrusts the knife into the air above the shaker. The blade is turned over so that the salt is now seen. It will appear that you have just caught the salt grains on the knife. (Be certain that none of your audience is too close when you quickly raise the knife.)

"There it is! The oxygen in the air combines with the metal and attracts the sodium chloride." Hand the salt shaker to the spectator and wipe the knife with the napkin. *"Would you like to try it?"* Hand him the knife.

If a nice amount of salt sticks to the blade you might combine this trick with the preceding trick, Osmo-Salt. After you have caught the salt on the knife, pretend to pour it into your left hand. You can then cause it to penetrate the napkin as in the previous trick. By doing one effect after another in a logical sequence you develop what is known as a routine. Combine a few tricks in this way, so that they follow one another in an entertaining manner.

DOT'S DOT

The versatility of the paddle move is endless. While still on the subject of tricks with salt we will continue to use a knife as our tool. Later we will discuss the use of other objects. In this illusion the spectators are allowed to see that water makes the salt stick to the knife, since it is part of the magic. Consequently, you will be wise not to do either of the two previous effects at the same sitting.

Wet your finger and place two small drops of water on the blade of your knife. Pour salt on each one and shake away the excess. Turn the knife over and add two more drops in the same position, so these dots are directly over the first two. Add the salt. You now have two salt dots on each side of the blade.

"This is a puzzle I could never understand." Show the dots on both sides. The knife is held as before in readiness for the paddle move. *"If I take away these two spots . . ."* Bring the knife between your left thumb and forefinger. The left forefinger goes under the knife, the thumb covers the top spot (Figure 16). With a rubbing motion your thumb removes the top spot. Your index finger below the blade moves back and forth but *does not* touch the spot. Turn the knife over using the paddle move. *". . . two spots are left, one on each side."*

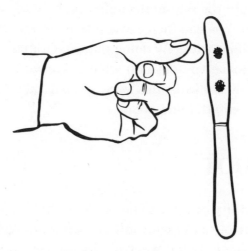

Figure 16

Pretend to rub away the remaining salt spots on top and bottom of the blade. The top spot is actually removed while the bottom one remains. The paddle move again will convince the spectators that the blade now is clean. *"If I take away the last two spots, nothing is left."* (You actually have two spots hidden under the blade.)

"This is the part I can't figure out. If I wave the knife back and forth a few times"—move the hand from right to left—*"the spots seem to come back."* Turn the knife over *without* doing the paddle move. The spots have returned. Repeat the paddle move and show spots on both sides of the blade. *"If I take away only the top spots"*—rub them away with your flat forefinger—*"the bottom spots disappear also."*

Hand the knife to the nearest spectator. *"I don't know why it happens, but dot's dot!"*

THREE QUICK ONES

These are not strictly magic but fall into the category of table tricks. All of them involve salt.

Separating Pepper from Salt Pour a small amount of salt onto the table. Now pour some pepper into the palm of your hand. Sparingly pinch some grains of pepper from your hand, dropping them onto the salt pile. You will now claim that you can remove the pepper from the salt in three seconds. To accomplish this you'll need a pocket comb. Run the comb through your hair a few times to pick up some static electricity. Pass the comb over the salt and watch the pepper grains jump up into the teeth. The salt pile will be clean. Instead of using your hair, you can also rub the comb on your sleeve if your coat is made of wool or fur.

Instant Separation Pour some salt onto a business card or small piece of paper. (The dinner check will work if you want to bet to see who pays it.) Add an equal amount of pepper and mix the two together with your finger. You can bet that you can separate the salt from the pepper with a single twist of your wrist. To win the bet, merely twist the paper over a glass of water so that all the grains slide off. The salt goes to the bottom while the pepper floats on top. Hand the spectator your dinner check.

Ice-cube Suspension   If you have a piece of string in your pocket you can lift an ice cube from a glass of water. Touch the string to the top of the ice cube so that the end of the string coils a turn or two. Sprinkle some salt on top of the string and ice cube, and wait a moment for the ice to melt. Keep the string in place. In a few seconds the ice cube will refreeze and will imbed the string. You will then be able to lift the string and bring the ice cube out of the glass.

SUGAR FLOATS

Finding a restaurant that still serves lump sugar is one of the most difficult tricks you can do nowadays. Whenever I find one I can't resist doing some magic at dinner. One of the most unusual stunts is performed when the coffee arrives.

When your coffee is poured, and before you add cream, quietly slip a sugar cube into the cup so that it stands upright. The cube won't be seen since it is covered by the coffee. Pick up another lump and turn it sideways. *"Did you know that sugar will float only in South American coffee, not in other kinds?"* Place the lump in your cup so that it rests on the hidden cube, forming a T shape (Figure 17).

The top lump will appear to float. *"This must be South American coffee."* In a few moments the hot coffee will melt the support, so be ready to command the cube to sink. *"That's enough. You can sink now."* If you time the words correctly the sugar mysteriously disappears in the cup. If the coffee is very hot the bottom lump will melt too fast, so allow it to cool for a few minutes before you begin your trick.

SOFT SPOT

A logical adult is more easily fooled than the youngster who has not as yet developed numerous preconceived ideas. Our minds are conditioned to accept without question the things we see around us every day. A magician plays tricks on the mind as well as the eye when he tampers with an ordinary object. Here is an example of the kind of chicanery that fools with logic.

In a bowl filled with cubes of sugar it is logical to assume that every wrapper in fact contains sugar. At some opportune time during dinner steal a lump of sugar and bring it into your lap. Unwrap it very carefully. Remove the sugar and repack the empty wrapper so that it still has its original shape. Put the empty shell back into the sugar bowl. Leave the sugar in your lap.

Knock on various parts of the table with your knuckles. This establishes that the table is solid. *"Is this a solid table?*

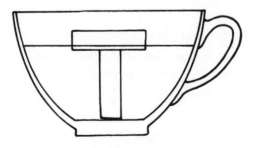

Figure 17

I'll bet it's not." Rap the table a few times in front of you until you settle on a spot about a foot in front of you. *"Every table has a soft spot, you know. Aha. Here it is. The soft spot."* Allow a few spectators to rap on the same spot. *"I'm sure this is it. Let's mark it."*

Pick up the empty sugar package and set it on the spot you just selected. *"May I have that glass?"* Take an empty glass and set it on top of the shell. The shell has the right shape to support a light glass. A logical mind is now assured that there is sugar in the package—otherwise it would flatten out from the weight.

"Please hold your hand above the glass." As soon as he does this, your hand goes on top of his and presses down sharply to startle the poor spectator. *"Look! We just flattened the sugar."* Lift the glass and flip the empty paper toward the spectator. *"It went right through the table. I knew there was a soft spot there."* As you are speaking move your right hand all the way under the table to a point directly below the soft spot. Bring the hand out again, picking up the sugar from your lap and dropping it onto the table. *"Isn't that a sweet trick?"*

SLAP IT THROUGH

One of the regulars at the Magicians' Table at Rosoff's Restaurant is a man named Larry Arcuri, who has been an officer in the Society of American Magicians for many years. When he sees lump sugar you can almost bet that he will do this effect.

Steal a lump of sugar from the bowl and remove the wrapper as you did in the previous trick. Place the empty package back in the bowl and wait for your coffee. When you have the spectator's attention you ask, *"Do you take sugar in your coffee?"*

Pick up the empty shell with the right hand, hiding the actual sugar lump in your left hand with your thumb. *"I hate these packages—they take so much time to unwrap. Luckily I'm a magician. This is the way a magician puts sugar in his coffee."* Place the wrapper on the back of your left hand. Hold your hand over the coffee cup. Your right fingers slap the shell, crushing it flat against the hand. At the same time open your left hand and allow the sugar to drop into the coffee (Figure 18). Pick up a spoon and start to stir your coffee. *"I hope it melts quickly, or I'll go stir-crazy."*

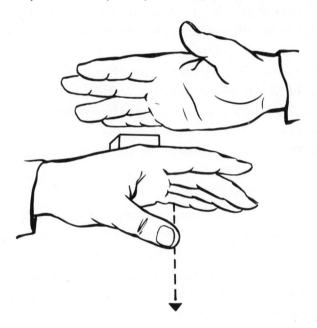

Figure 18

SUGAR TRANSFER

Lump sugar has a remarkable quality which has been used by magicians for many years. Write a letter or number on a lump of sugar using a pencil. Press your thumb against the sugar, and the writing is transferred to your thumb. You can now do some offset printing by pressing your thumb to a menu or flat surface. Using this knowledge we can create some startling effects. Try this one.

A pencil and lump of sugar are in your lap. Ask the spectator to call out any number from one to ten. Let us assume he or she calls out *"Seven."* Magicians have learned this is the number which is most often selected.

Once you hear the number, write it boldly on the sugar. Do not look down as you write. Have your spectator place an ashtray on top of a drinking glass in the center of the table. Having some ashes in the tray is important. Press your thumb firmly against the cube and get the transfer. Bring your hand onto the table.

"What was that number again?" It is named again, and you request that the spectator *"Lift the ashtray and put your hand on the glass."* As he does this you add, *"No, the other hand."* As you speak, take the ashtray from the spectator's hand and press your thumb against his palm. Place that palm over the glass and set the ashtray on top of his hand. You have printed the number on his or her palm.

Pick up a knife and use the point to scratch a seven into the ashes. *"There is your number seven. Did you feel anything strange just then?"* No matter what the reply you command, *"Look at your hand!"*

Back in your lap, quietly rub the telltale mark off your thumb.

TRANSFER VARIATION

Our magic concentrates on two important objectives. First, we must keep the execution of each trick simple. Second, we should make the conclusion effective and dramatic. We know how simple the transfer principle is to perform. Now let's build on it to get the most powerful effect we can.

In this case every move will be done directly on the table. Select a lump of sugar and unwrap it openly for all to see. Remove a pencil from your pocket. Hand the sugar and the pencil to the spectator at your right or your left. Set a glass of water in front of the spectator.

"I want you to clear your mind. Please think of any number, letter of the alphabet, or geometric design—any one that comes to mind most easily." When your spectator affirms that he or she has done this, you continue: *"Take the pencil and very boldly and firmly draw that design or number on the sugar cube. Make it as dark and legible as you can."* Wait until this has been done. *"Place the cube on the table so that we can all see what you have chosen to draw."* Move the glass a bit closer to your subject. *"Please open your right hand."*

When the subject has done this, pick up the cube of sugar so that your thumb presses against the drawing to pick up the transfer. Do not hesitate but continue the action of handing the cube to the spectator. *"Please drop the sugar into the glass of water."* As he is doing this, pick up the spectator's other hand transferring your mark to his palm.

Continue to lift the hand, offering instructions: *"This hand goes on top of the glass so that no one can put anything in or take anything out."* The dirty work is all done.

"Please watch the particles of graphite as they rise from the sugar. I shall not touch you, but I will merely place my hand above yours." Do this by holding your hand a few inches above the spectator's hand. The use of the phrase, *"I shall not touch you,"* is a psychological ploy. When the trick is over the spectator will swear that you did not touch him or her. *"Watch the graphite. Do you feel anything strange?"*

Snap your fingers over the hand very dramatically. *"There. It is done!"* Move away from the spectator. *"Open your hand!"* The imprint will be very plain on the palm, and there are a few grains of graphite floating in the water.

This dramatic trick might be used as the final climax of your dinner-table show. It will be long remembered.

SUGAR QUICK TRICKS

A few table stunts are always in order. Here are some performed with sugar.

Catching Your Lumps Hold a lump of sugar against the side of a glass with your thumb. Add another lump on top of the first one (Figure 19). Holding the whole thing in one hand, offer to bet that you can toss each lump into the glass, one at a time. But let your table companion try it first—he may think this is simple, but it is not. Each time he tries it the first lump will fly out of the glass as he tries to toss up the second lump.

The secret is simple. Toss up the first lump and catch it. The second time, you do not throw the sugar into the air, but instead release your thumb and bring the glass under the falling cube.

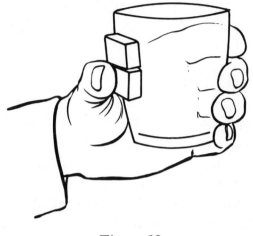

Figure 19

Burning a Cube   Challenge the spectator to light the end of a sugar cube so that it will blaze. He cannot do it. You can—by rubbing the edge of the cube into some ashes from the ashtray. The ashes will start it burning, and the alcohol in the sugar will then keep it going.

Turnover   Place four cubes of sugar in a row on the table. You will turn around and a spectator will turn one lump over. When you turn back to the table you name the correct lump.

How? Easy—while you are quietly laying out the lumps, sprinkle a bit of salt on top of each one. When the spectator turns the sugar over, the salt spills off. He will not notice this since the salt and sugar look the same. You then tap each one to see where the salt is missing.

Dinner-roll Diversions

LIGHT BREAD

Most people don't associate dinner rolls with magicians, but you will discover you can use almost any handy object for your miracles. You also will find that some basic principles can be adapted to numerous tricks. The Flying Spoon illusion described earlier can be adapted for use with a dinner roll. Present it this way:

Open a dinner napkin and set it on the table loosely draped in front of you. The two ends should be handy so that you can raise the napkin like a curtain in front of you. Hidden under the top fold on the right is your trusty dinner fork. The tines point to the left. A breadbasket of dinner rolls is in the center of the table.

When you are ready to perform, lift the napkin by taking each end between the thumb and middle fingers. The fork is secretly held behind the napkin at your right. Lift the napkin straight up and angle the fork down toward the center (Figure 20).

Drape the entire napkin over the basket of dinner rolls. The center of the napkin should be over the top roll. Once all the bread is covered, secretly push the tines of the fork into the top dinner roll, holding the napkin securely. Exerting pressure with the right thumb will cause the roll to move eerily behind the cloth.

"I'm on a diet and can only eat light foods. I'll need the lightest roll." Lift your hands and the roll will appear to

levitate away from the basket. Bring the hands up and move your arms forward. Stand up as though the roll were pulling you from the seat. Start slowly and move the roll with care. You can then move it back and forth or up and down a few times as though it were quite active.

Lower the roll toward the edge of the table near you. As it settles on the table, hold the top of the roll through the cloth. Your left hand does this with a fancy gesture for attention while your right hand dislodges the fork. As your right hand now gently pulls back toward your body, the fork drops into your lap and the napkin rides over the top of the roll. Shake it and toss the napkin aside. With both hands break the roll open, concealing any small holes that the fork made. *"This seems light enough for my diet."*

Figure 20

EASY COME, EASY DOUGH

In modern vernacular money is often called "bread." A person with plenty of "dough" is considered rich. If you like puns, as I do, you can have fun with the patter as well as the magic. But let's start with the trick and discuss the patter later. There are three ways in which to present this effect.

Hold a coin in your right hand. A quarter or half dollar is best, but a smaller coin will do. No one is watching carefully at this time, so don't make any great effort to hide the coin. It should rest on your middle and ring fingers near the second joint. Your left hand draws the attention by picking up the roll. The left thumb is on top with fingers underneath.

Bring your two hands together palm up, pressing the coin directly under its side of the bun. Both thumbs join at the top. Break the roll in half by pressing upward with your fingers and outward with your thumbs (Figure 21). The right middle finger pushes the coin between the halves as you do this. Keep the bottom halves of the roll together for maximum effect. This will give the illusion that the coin was baked into the roll. Produce it and hold it up for all to see.

Figure 21

A second way to do this is as follows: the edge of a quarter or half dollar is pinched between the index and middle fingers of your right hand. The same hand takes the dinner roll so that the thumb is on top and fingers underneath. Push the coin upward, pressing it into the bottom of the bun. Put the roll down in front of you and brush both hands together as though you were getting rid of some crumbs. This shows your empty hands. Now break the roll open as before to expose the coin.

If you have a chance to steal the roll beforehand, try this method. Fold a dollar bill in half lengthwise and roll it into a small package. Poke your finger into the bottom of the roll. Now push the rolled-up bill into the hole you just made. Make sure that you don't push it too far, or you'll come through the top. Put the roll back into the breadbasket and wait for the right moment to produce the money the same way as before.

The patter is important to call attention to the roll and to give you an excuse for opening it. Here are a few different ways in which to present the effect.

"I love to eat here. The chef is a friend of mine, and he bakes special goodies for me. Here is one of them." Break open the roll and produce your money.

"Have you ever listened to a couple of mod youngsters talking about money? 'Man, I really need some bread.' I've often wondered why they use that expression. To them, bread means money." Produce the money. *"To me too!"*

"I have an uncle who's a baker. He makes a lot of dough. Well, he really kneads it. He lives in the East. I'll bet you think I have a lot of crust to tell a crumby story like that. But when I say dough, I don't mean dough." Pick up your roll, break it open to show the money. *"I mean dough!"*

ONCE IN A KNIFETIME

This can be a most startling production when presented properly. Do it as casually as possible, with no special buildup. Words will not help here.

Slip a dinner knife under the watchband on your left wrist. The knife should be pointed toward your fingers. The tip should rest just below the base of the ring finger (Figure 22). Use a butter knife or one that is not too sharp, so as not to cut yourself on the point. Your left arm rests on the table, palm down, concealing the knife.

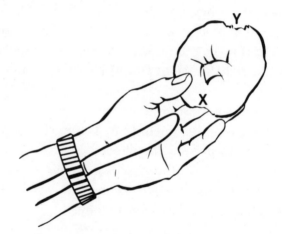

Figure 22

"May I have that roll, please?" Your right index finger points to the roll. As you take the roll your middle finger secretly pokes a hole in the bottom (X). Place the roll between the thumb and forefinger of your left hand as in the diagram, turning your entire body to the right. The back of your arm is facing the person opposite you.

Pinch a bit of the bread from the top of the roll (Y). Eat it. *"I'll need a knife for this one."* Reach into the top of the roll. A turn of your left wrist will bring the tip of the knife into proper alignment. The tip goes right into the small hole. Insert your fingers in the hole you pinched, take the tip, and pull it out from the top very slowly until the entire knife is revealed. Draw it out in an upward motion.

"May I have the butter, please?" Butter your roll and enjoy the reactions of your spectators. If there are breadsticks on the table, you can substitute one of them for the knife. Pull it out of the roll, remarking, *"This is some high-class restaurant. They have bread in their bread."*

You can see that this trick is very easy to adapt to objects, like a pencil or pen. Before signing your dinner check, take a pen out of your dinner roll and watch the expression on your waiter's face.

CLINGING BREADSTICK

This very old stunt is usually done by a magician using a wand, but any long object can be used. In the event that someone in your audience has seen it before or knows the principle, we have added a "sucker" finish.

Place a breadstick vertically across your left palm. It is resting along the base of your fingers, with your thumb holding it in place. Turn your palm toward your body; bring your right hand up to the left wrist. Position your fingers around the wrist as in the diagram. The thumb is on top, the middle finger, ring finger and pinky around the other side. The index finger is extended into the palm and rests on the breadstick holding it in place (Figures 23 and 24).

"Watch how the breadstick clings to my fingers." Lift your left thumb away from the palm. The stick appears to adhere to your hand. Shake your hand up and down, and it will not fall off. Take your right hand away and make a grabbing catch at the stick.

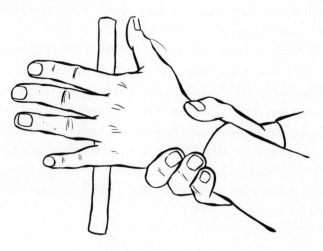

Figure 23

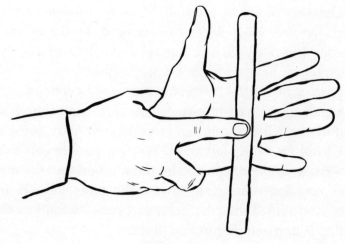

Figure 24

The trick is complete at this point. You will find, however, that many people know this principle from their childhood days. If you hear a comment like *"That's an easy one. Anybody can do it,"* get ready for the sucker finish.

Challenge the spectator to explain it. If he does so correctly, suggest that he demonstrate the trick his way.

As he is doing this, secretly slip a knife under your watchband as in the Once in a Knifetime trick. Now you pick up the breadstick and go through the same motions as before. But this time wedge it between the knife and your palm. The knife performs the same function as your index finger did before. *"When you get your breadstick to stand up straight, remember never to take the other hand away."* As you speak, you take your right hand away and the stick is still clinging to the hand. Take it from your left hand and offer it to your wiseguy. *"Care to try it my way?"* Get rid of the knife in your lap.

Like other tricks covered so far, you can vary the objects you use. Instead of a breadstick you can use a knife, long pencil, comb, or even a stalk of celery or a carrot. Just have fun with it.

CRACKER STORY

Adding some social comment to your magic makes for variety. While telling this sad story, use a small square soda cracker—the kind that is usually served with soup. Borrow a lipstick from one of the women or use a felt marking pen to write on the cracker.

"Did you ever try to return merchandise to a busy department store after a holiday sale? Let me show you what happened to me."

Pick up a cracker and draw an arrow on one side. The arrow points up. Turn the cracker over to your left, as if turning the page of a book. Draw another arrow so that it points to your right (Figure 25).

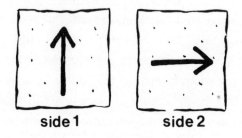

side 1   side 2

Figure 25

Your left index finger and thumb hold the cracker as shown in Figure 26. The index finger at A is positioned diagonally across from the thumb (D). You can see the arrow pointing upward, but the person opposite you will see the arrow pointing to his right.

"I was in the store looking for the returns department. I saw a sign that pointed to the right, so I went to the right."

Push the cracker at point B away from you. Use your right index finger. This pivots the cracker so that B and C change places. The arrow will still look the same to the spectator.

"I followed the sign around the building." Pivot the cracker twice in the same way. *"And I wound up in the same place as I started."* Take the cracker with your right hand. Your right index finger and thumb hold the cracker at points B and C. This time your left index finger will pivot at position A (Figure 26).

"I asked the floor manager for help. He pointed in one

direction, while the store detective showed me the other way." Pivot a few times. The arrows will vary from right to left each time (spectator's view). End up with the up arrow facing you. Put the cracker back into its original position in your left hand.

"*Now I was really confused, so I went downstairs.*" Turn the cracker so that your view shows the arrow pointing to the left. The spectator sees a down arrow.

"*I found a clerk who asked me to fill out a form and take it upstairs.*" Pivot again. "*I got upstairs and another clerk initialed the form and sent me down again.*" Pivot. "*I went up again to validate it and down again to get the numbers approved.*" Pivot twice more. "*This took two and a half hours. And then they hit me with the sad news. It wasn't their merchandise. I was in the wrong store!*"

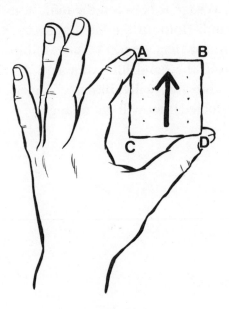

Figure 26

Turn the cracker so that the arrow faces down (your view). *"I went straight to my car"*—pivot a few more times—*"and went to pieces!"* Break the cracker by crushing it in your palm, sprinkling the crumbs into the ashtray.

BREAD GAGS

Hard Rolls Have a coin in your hand under the table. Pick up a dinner roll and softly rap it on the table. At the same time knock the coin against the table from underneath. *"This must be a very hard roll."*

Biting a Finger While your party is waiting to be served, break a breadstick so that it is about as long as your middle finger. Wedge it between the middle and ring fingers of your left hand. Hold up the hand and announce, *"I'm so hungry I can eat my finger."* Take a bite out of the breadstick. Bring the hand into your lap. At first glance it appears that you are really biting a finger. Even if the audience isn't fooled, you will get a laugh.

Napkin Hocus-pocus

SPOOKY

When asked to perform my favorite napkin trick, this is the one I choose. It is a fun trick and one that people talk about. Use a cloth napkin for it.

"That's a very nice tie. It's made of those spooky threads." Say that to a gentleman at your table. *"Some threads have spooky fibers. I'll show you."* Reach for the end of his necktie. Hold the bottom between your thumb and

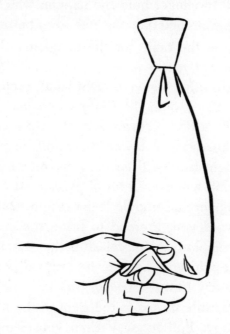

Figure 27

forefinger (Figure 27). While your right hand pretends to pull some thread from the tip of the tie, your left middle finger will move up and down rapidly three times. Pause and do it again. Both actions are simultaneous. For every single pull with your right hand, your left middle finger moves up and down.

The effect is quite comical—it will look as though you were unraveling his tie. *"There! I think I have enough of the spooky stuff."* Hold your hands apart as though you were holding a real piece of thread between them. Carefully set the imaginary thread on the table. *"Keep an eye on that, will you?"*

Pick up your dinner napkin by one corner. Place it in your left hand and pull the end up through your left fist so that four or five inches are showing at the top (Figure 28). Your left thumb and forefinger hold the napkin, which will stand up quite erect. Starched napkins look even better.

Pretend to look on the table for the imaginary thread. *"Those spook fibers are really hard to see, aren't they?"* Pretend to find it and, using just your right hand, pretend to tie it to the tip of the napkin. *"Luckily I can make one-handed knots."* Make a few gestures over the tip and then draw the imaginary thread back toward your body about five inches or so. Your right hand will now tug on the imaginary thread. The left thumb will exert a bit of pressure at a point between the index finger and middle finger (Figure 29). The napkin will tip toward you. Pretend to bring the invisible thread toward the napkin again, relaxing the left thumb pressure, and the napkin goes back to its original position. Repeat this action a few times. *"Spooky, isn't it?"*

Now take the invisible thread to the front of the napkin, away from your body. Pull it away from you. Move the thumb upward, pressing it against the upper edge of the

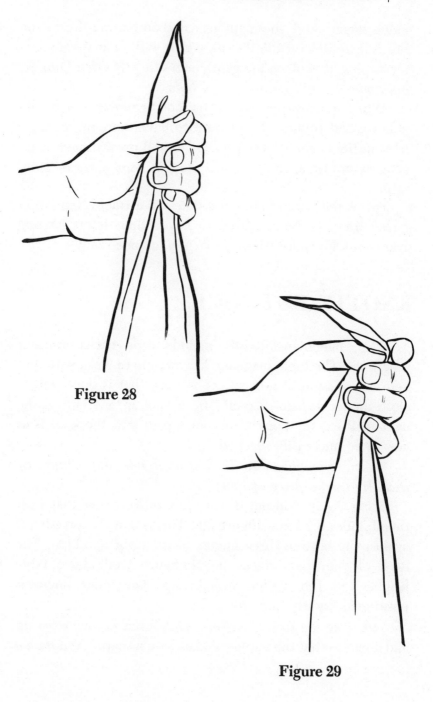

Figure 28

Figure 29

index finger, and the napkin will bend away from you. Pretend to pick off the thread, wet it with your tongue, and try to press it back on the gentleman's tie. *"If I don't put this back your tie will unravel in an hour."*

When moving the napkin try not to move your hand— only the left thumb. If you want to have some more laughs later in the evening, wet your finger and press it against the gentleman's tie again. *"Sorry. I thought I saw your tie going again."*

This is the type of nonsense that will attract attention in a restaurant, so be prepared to have other diners coming over to ask for more tricks—have a quick one ready.

KNOTTY BUT NICE

Stage magicians usually include rope tricks in their repertoire. The table magician has no rope to work with, but here is a version of a classic rope trick that is done with a cloth dinner napkin. Secretly tie a knot in one end of the napkin. Place the napkin in your lap so that the knot is at your right and easily reached.

"I saw a magician on TV last week who did a fantastic trick. He used a piece of rope."

Bring the napkin out of your lap, making sure that your thumb hides the knot (Figure 30). This is done by pressing it against the bottom three fingers of the right hand (A). The back of your hand faces the audience well above table height. Lift the napkin straight up. The index finger is positioned slightly forward.

"He gave the rope one good shake." Shake your wrist up and down so that the napkin shakes with a snap. *"And then a*

few more." This time bring the bottom of the napkin up (B), pinching it between your index and middle fingers (X). Shake your hand and let the bottom (B) drop. So far there has been no change. On the third try you will bring the bottom up again. Do not let it drop this time, but hold on to it firmly. Allow the knot to drop by relaxing the pressure of your thumb. It should look as though you just knotted the napkin by shaking it. *"And then he had a knot in the rope. I sure wish I knew how he did it. I would love to do that one."*

Figure 30

PERSIAN PUPPET

Use this one as a follow-up to the Knotty but Nice trick, using the same napkin with a knot in one end. This stunt will add fun to your act, especially if there are small children at the dinner table.

"Ancient Persian magicians used to perform an outstanding illusion in the middle of the desert. They would build a small tent." Place a large dinner menu in front of you to act as a screen. *"The magician would make a few magical passes over the tent."* Hold the top of your knotted napkin over the screen. Now dip it behind the menu. The moment it is out of sight, place your left index finger in the knot. Open your palm so that the napkin forms a sort of cape around the back of your hand (Figure 31). Extend your left thumb and middle fingers. These will act as the arms of a small puppet. Drape the folds of the napkin around the little arms, holding it in place with your bottom two fingers (Figure 32).

"A real live Persian would appear." Blow on the menu so that it falls flat on the table. The puppet moves and takes a bow. *"Are you a real live Persian?"* Have the puppet shake his head by moving your index finger from side to side. *"You're not? What are you?"* Bring the puppet to your ear and pretend to hear him. *"He says he's a Persian puppet."* You can now have some fun with him, making him clap hands, wave, or pick up table objects.

TRANSPO-KNOTS

Either of these two components can be performed as individual tricks. When you put them together you have

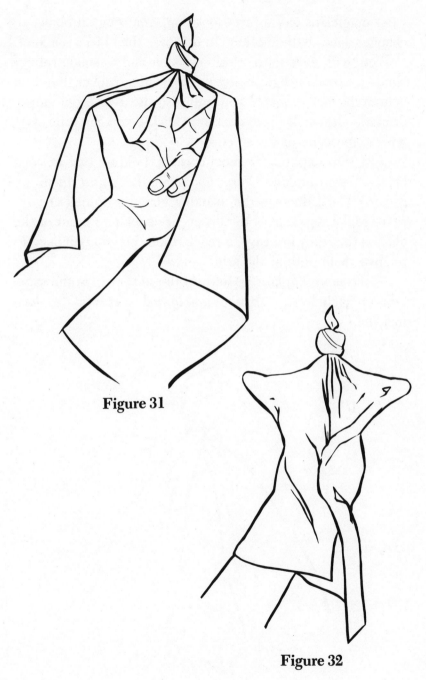

Figure 31

Figure 32

what magicians call a "transposition"—causing an object to change places with another. In this case the object is a knot.

You will need four cloth napkins and a small rubber band—preferably light-colored. Keep the rubber band in your right coat pocket. You will also use two large empty drinking glasses. If these are not available you can improvise with soup dishes or coffee cups.

Lift two napkins by their corners, holding one in each hand. *"Two napkins. Very lonesome. Let's put them to-gether."* Place them in the drinking glass positioned at your right. Make sure that both corners are sticking up out of the glass so that they are easy to reach. Later on you will need to remove them both at the same time.

"Two more napkins." Hold up the next pair in the same fashion as before. *"They're lonely too. Let me tie them together."*

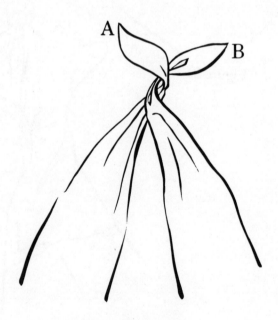

Figure 33

Twist the corners of the napkins one around the other as in Figure 33. Corners A and B are then tied into a simple knot (Figure 34). If you examine it carefully you will see that there is really no knot at all; but to the spectator it will seem as though you have tied a square knot. Place the false knot into the empty glass at your left. Poke the napkins in after it, gently.

"We now have two napkins that have a knot"—point to the glass at your left—*"and two that have not"*—point to the glass at your right. *"We'll need a sprinkle of magic powder."*

As you say this put both hands into your pockets. The right hand takes the rubber band so that it is wrapped around the tips of your thumb and three middle fingers. Your left hand comes out of your left pocket first and pretends to sprinkle some powder on the napkins, left and then right. Your right hand is now on the table. Be casual so as not to

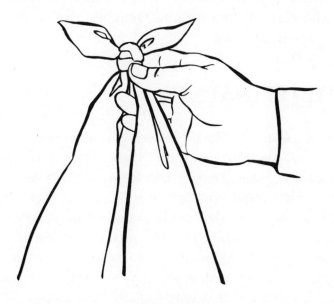

Figure 34

call attention to the rubber band. *"The magic is done."* Your right hand picks up the ends of the napkins in the right-hand glass. At the same time you secretly slip the rubber band around both ends and toss the napkin gently into the air. *"These two are now knotted."*

Your left hand immediately removes the two napkins from the left glass by shaking them gently one at a time. They will come out of the glass separated. *"While these are not!"* As you hold up the napkins in your left hand, your right hand secretly rolls the rubber band off the other napkins. Put all four napkins together. *"When is a knot not a knot? When it is not!"* Separate the napkins and drop them on the table one at a time.

As mentioned earlier, you can use the knotting and unknotting as separate tricks. If you tie two napkins together as described you can toss them into the air and they mysteriously untie. Conversely, if you add the rubber band to two napkins before you toss them into the air, they come down apparently tied.

UTILITY NAPKIN

You might consider it flattering to have people ask you the same question again and again: *"Can you make me disappear?"* (After hearing this for over thirty-five years, I often wish I could.) But we must remember that magicians are associated in the public mind with making things disappear. You should be able to do it at the drop of a napkin. Using the following method you can "vanish," as we put it, almost any small object that will fit in your hand. For this example we will assume you are using an olive.

Open your dinner napkin squarely on the table in front of

you. Fold the napkin in half by taking the two bottom ends and folding them up to meet the two top corners. Now fold the napkin in half again, bringing the right side to the left. All the corners meet at your left. Pick up the four corners with your left thumb on top and your left middle finger underneath. You will see that you have formed a small bag. Bring your left index finger around toward you. It takes the place of the thumb, which moves away from the bag.

Your right hand picks up the olive. Your whole hand goes into the back pocket of the bag, the part nearest you, between sections 1 and 2 in Figure 35. Put your hand all the way down into the pocket. Do not let go of the olive. It is held against the palm with your pinky and middle fingers.

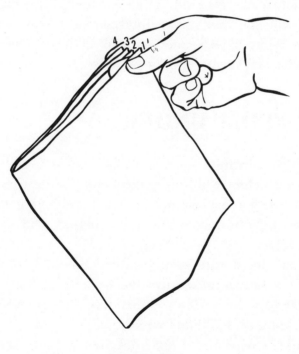

Figure 35

Your right hand comes up and almost out of the bag. The thumb and index fingers grasp the corners as shown in Figure 35. Thumb is positioned at number 1, with the index finger behind number 4. Your middle finger remains at the top of the bag between sections 1 and 2. It is touching the thumb through the cloth.

Your left hand now comes away from the bag. It should look as though you are merely transferring the bag from left to right hand.

Lift the bag upward and shake your wrist. As you snap the cloth, remove your index finger and the napkin will drop open. The olive remains concealed behind the cloth. Your left hand picks up one of the fallen ends. Open the napkin and as you drape it flat on the table, allow the olive to fall quietly into your lap. Fold the napkin and set it aside.

You will find that this method works equally well with other everyday objects, such as book matches, coins, small salt shakers and sugar cubes or packets.

OUT FROM UNDER

For this startling vanish you will need a "confederate." Your secret helper will do the dirty work while you get the applause, so choose a person who won't mind not getting the attention. Equally important, find a helper who will keep your secret.

Several people are seated around the table. You have already learned to make any object vanish, as long as it is small enough to be held in your hand. In this case we will use a small shot glass half filled with liquid.

"I had a request for this trick. It was my doctor who

requested it. He told me not to drink anymore. So I don't. I don't drink any less—but certainly not any more." Pick up the small glass and hold it just below your eye level. With your other hand drape a cloth napkin over the glass so that the center of the napkin covers the mouth.

"*Would you please verify that the glass is actually under the cloth.*" Move the glass and napkin to a spectator nearby. He is to reach under the cloth and feel the glass. You are still holding on to the bottom of the glass. Offer another spectator the same option. "*Will you please check to see that the glass is, in fact, under the cloth.*"

Now offer the glass to a third spectator—your secret helper. The glass is held just high enough so that the bottom of the napkin touches the table. Move the glass toward you as the napkin hangs slightly over the edge of the table. Your helper reaches underneath and takes the glass away, bringing it down to his or her lap. Your fingers imitate the shape of the glass underneath the cloth. Hold up the tips of your thumb, index, and middle fingers in a triangular shape to create the illusion.

With a dramatic, sudden gesture throw the napkin into the air above the table. It comes down with a flutter. The liquid and glass are gone! "*That's one way to avoid drinking.*"

Drape the cloth over the fingers, held in the triangular shape as before, and turn to your helper. "*Put your hand under the cloth and see what you find.*" Bring the bottom of the napkin directly over the confederate's lap. He or she will bring the glass up under the cloth and into your fingers. At that moment you pull the napkin away, revealing the glass. Your helper should now act very surprised, perhaps remarking, "*I don't believe it.*"

Take your bow. Remember, you can use any object for this good trick. Money, salt shakers, wristwatches, or other small articles will vanish in the same manner.

TORN AND RESTORED NAPKIN

For centuries magicians have been fascinating audiences with the "restoration" effect: an object is destroyed and then made whole again. History records that about 2900 B.C. the Egyptian magician Dedi performed this one for King Cheops, builder of the famed pyramids. Dedi cut the head off a goose and with magical words restored the bird again. In the early fifteenth century a German girl was charged with witchcraft. She had been seen to tear a handkerchief into many pieces and then reconstruct it.

Since that time there have been a great many variations of the trick. You have probably seen decapitation tricks with guillotines, or ladies sawn in half. Simpler versions are often performed, such as cutting and restoring a piece of rope.

Another simple version is one we will do using a paper napkin. This method, using the Lap Vanish, is very direct and one that you will recognize. The mechanics are the same as you previously used with a package of sugar.

Unfold a paper napkin and then crumple it into a compact little ball, which you will secretly retain in your lap until needed. Now you are set to perform your miracle.

"May I have your napkin, please?" Take your spectator's paper napkin and unfold it carefully. Hold it up by the ends to display the entire napkin. *"Can you see the grain in the paper? The grain determines how it tears. For example, if I do it this way, it tears easily."* Tear the napkin in half as neatly as possible and place one half on top of the other. Turn the

papers to the right and tear them in half again. *"If I tear this way, it's a bit more difficult."*

Crumple all four pieces into a tight little ball that resembles the one in your lap. Place the ball about six inches in front of you on the table. Your right hand casually drops to your lap and picks up the extra ball. It is held loosely at the base of the bottom fingers.

"May I have the salt, please?"

This is the important misdirection. Here is what must happen: your left hand moves to the middle of the table, and your index finger points to the salt shaker. At the same time your right hand comes up from your lap and places its package directly in front of the torn napkin—the back of your hand will hide the ball. The right pinky is resting on the table. Do not hesitate. Your right hand slides back toward

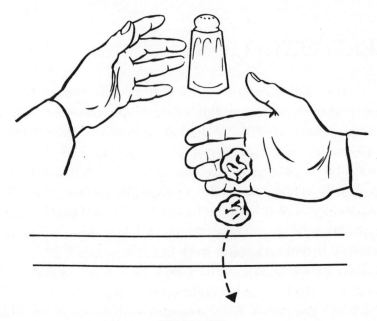

Figure 36

the edge of the table and pushes the torn pieces into your lap. Without pausing, move your hand forward, bringing it to rest in the center of the table, and lifting it to reveal the paper ball. The action should be smooth and continuous. The move should look as though you were merely picking up the pieces and placing them in the center of the table (Figure 36).

Sprinkle a bit of salt on the ball. *"The chloride in the salt tightens the molecules of the paper—it acts like a glue. You may not believe that, but the only alternative is to believe that this is magic."* Open the napkin gently so as not to tear it.

This Lap Vanish will be used for other tricks later. It does not require any skill but should be practiced so that it feels natural to you. A word of caution: *Never look down* when dropping any object into the lap.

TELEPORTATION

I learned this marvelous trick from a very dear friend who performed all over the world under the stage name Amedeo. Amedeo recently died at eighty-four, having been in show business for seventy of those years. He had played in twenty-three countries and was able to do his act in six languages. While primarily a stage performer, Amedeo occasionally played in nightclubs, where he did dinner-table magic. The trick you are about to learn was one of his favorites. It will take some work but it is worthwhile.

Two paper napkins are openly folded into squares of about four inches each. Four empty sugar packages are rolled into tight little balls. You can also use more colorful little packages of sugar substitutes. If neither is available make some little balls out of another piece of paper napkin. Roll them all the same way so that they look alike. All of this is done in front of your spectators as you tell your story.

"Let me tell you about four friends of mine who graduated from college and moved to different parts of the country."

As you talk you will be placing each of the balls on the table about eight inches apart, forming a square (Figure 37).

"One fellow lived up north in Oregon." Place the first paper ball in position 1 on the table.

"The second fellow lived in California." The second ball is placed at position 3.

"The third fellow went to live in Maine." Next ball at position 2.

"And the last man liked the warm climate in Florida." Place the last ball at position 4.

"Occasionally they spoke to one another on the phone." Hold a napkin square in each hand. Thumb is on top and

1

2

3

4

Figure 37

fingers are underneath. The left napkin covers the ball at position 3; the right napkin covers the ball at 4. *"When these two spoke, the other two didn't."*

Move the napkins up to cover numbers 1 and 2. *"If these two spoke, the other two didn't."* Secretly clip the ball at position 2 between the middle and ring fingers of the right hand. This is best done by separating the two fingers under the napkin (Figure 38). *"When these two spoke, the others were left out."* The left napkin now comes over position 2. It will overlap the right napkin. At that moment draw your right-hand napkin down to cover position 4. Leave both napkins on the table in those positions. You have secretly taken the ball from 2 and added it to 4.

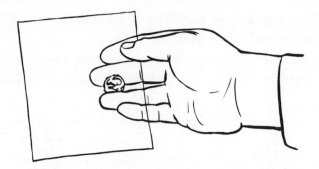

Figure 38. Note: Napkin is shown as though clear so that position of fingers can be seen.

"One day the fellows decided to have a reunion. The trouble was that they didn't have the fare to fly around the country. So, naturally, they phoned me. They knew that being a magician I could get them all together by teleportation. That's what I said—telepathic transportation, sometimes called teleportation. Here's how it works."

Your right hand picks up the exposed ball at position 1

and brings it under the table so that it is directly under 1, the Oregon position. Your fingernails tap the underside of the table for some noise. *"The fellow in Oregon merely concentrates on where he would like to be—Florida, in this case."* Your right hand remains under the table but moves so that it is directly under position 4. Your left hand lifts the napkin at that position and exposes the extra ball. All attention is centered on the two balls. Your left hand casually brings the napkin to your right hand as it comes out from under the table. The ball, which is clipped between your fingers as before, is hidden under the napkin. *"Teleportation is a cheap means of travel."*

Place the napkin back on the two balls. Now you secretly add the third one. *"Let's travel from California this time."* Repeat the steps by taking 3 and putting it under the table. Tap a few times for noise and again as your left hand lifts the napkin over 4, and your right hand moves back under it. Your left hand places the napkin into the right again, hiding the extra ball as you put it with the others. Cover 4 again.

Point to position 2 with your right index finger. *"The last fellow was a deep thinker. Not only could he teleport himself, but he could melt right through the cold atmosphere of Maine and wind up in the Florida sunshine."* Make a magical pass over both napkins before lifting them to expose the four balls in one pile.

For an extra "shock" you could use the Lap Vanish as you pretend to pick up all four balls and hand them to the spectator.

Hand him nothing as you remark, *"Here are the four of them, invisible but happily reunited."*

Keep in mind that this trick can be done with any small item that will not bulge under the napkin. You can use peanuts, raisins, or even small rolled-up balls of bread.

PRODUCING A RABBIT

Every magician needs a rabbit. (Even a bald magician can use a little hare.) You can make a cute dinner-table rabbit by folding a cloth napkin as described here.

The napkin is draped on the back of your right hand so that the sides hang evenly (Figure 39). The edge (C) is about two inches from the ends of your fingertips.

Your left hand tucks the cloth at C so it is held under your right thumb and three fingers. Your pinky is free (Figure 40).

Bring up corner A so that it goes across and in front of your fingertips. Tuck it in between your pinky and ring finger. Pull it up tight so that it looks like the ear of a rabbit. Bring corner B across and in front of your hand and tuck it between your thumb and index finger. Pull the ears up tight so they fit snugly in the crotch of your fingers (Figure 41).

Bring your thumb and little finger together under the other fingers so that by moving them up and down they look like the mouth of your bunny. Wrap any excess cloth around your wrist. Put the whole thing in the crook of your elbow, and make the little rabbit look alive by moving its head and mouth (Figure 42).

WHAT DOES IT LOOK LIKE?

No book of table tricks should exclude this delightful folding gag. It's fun to do and always brings a laugh. We are going to fold a napkin to look like a bra. Here's how.

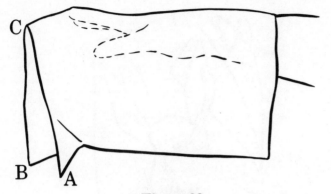

Figure 39

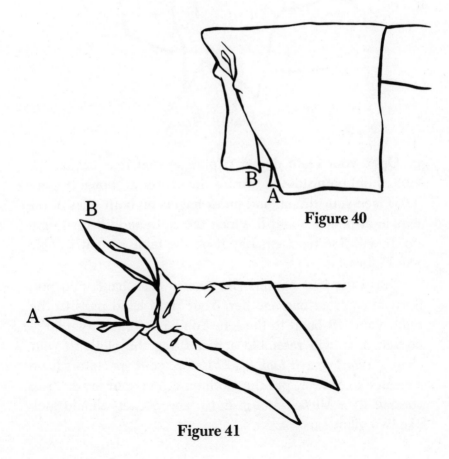

Figure 40

Figure 41

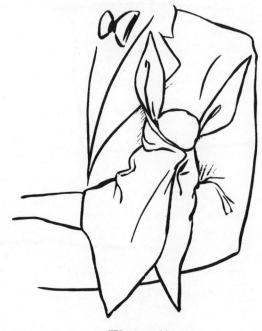

Figure 42

Open your cloth dinner napkin so that it is flat on the table. Fold both sides in toward the center as shown (Figure 43). Place your thumb and index fingers on both sides of the napkin at points A and B. Pinch the cloth and lift it straight up. It will fold by itself. Lay it on the table so that it looks like Figure 44.

Grasp the four corners (X), two in each hand, and pull them away from one another. Your right hand pulls to the right, your left hand to the left. You have formed two large pockets that will resemble a bra. Bring the cloth to your chest. *"What does it look like?"* Before your spectators have a chance to answer, put the cloth on top of your head. *"You guessed it—a Mickey Mouse hat!"* The pockets should look like two giant ears.

If you feel that you might embarrass anyone at the table, it is better not to do the stunt.

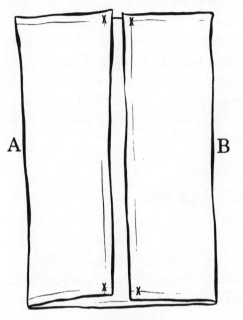

Figure 43

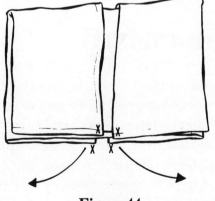

Figure 44

NAPKIN BETCHA

Place a twenty-five-cent piece on the table. Hand your spectator a paper napkin and say, *"You can't tear this napkin into four equal pieces with two tears. If you can do it, I'll give you a quarter."* The spectator can do this easily. So you lose, and you hand him a quarter: one of the four pieces he just tore. Pocket your coin.

STRONG PAPER

Twist a paper napkin diagonally from one corner to the other. Roll it very tightly so that it looks like a piece of rope. By pulling only the two ends your spectator cannot cause the napkin to break in the center. Have a few people try this.

But you can do it. While they are busy pulling, secretly wet your fingers. Take the napkin and touch your fingers to the center. This weakens the fibers so that the napkin will tear at that point.

NO MORE GRAVITY

A cloth napkin is placed over an empty drinking glass so that the center can be pushed down into the glass, forming a pocket. Pour water into the napkin and it will penetrate the cloth, filling the glass. Now draw the wet napkin around the glass. The napkin is outside the glass with the wet spot pulled taut on top of the glass. You can now turn the whole thing upside down and the water will seem to defy gravity. Right it quickly so it will not spill. Outside air pressure and surface tension keep the water inside.

WATCH IT GO!

With a bit of practice you can cause a cloth napkin to fly out of your hands like an arrow. Hold your napkin diagonally by opposite corners. Pull the right-hand corner very tightly and let it go with a snap. Your left hand releases its end at the same moment. The napkin should sail off to the right. Your right hand grabs for an end as it passes. *"There's a ghost in there, riding on a broomstick."*

COMEDY VANISH

Slydini is one of my favorite magicians. His sleight-of-hand ability and close-up magic win him acclaim by laymen and magicians alike. Slydini does a complete comedy act using the principle we are about to explain. In his hands this gag is a masterpiece.

Your spectator is seated, and you are standing at his left. A crumpled paper-napkin ball is in your right hand. Your left hand is extended palm up in front of him at about chin height. Show him the balled napkin, holding it directly in front of him. Place it into your left hand, counting, *"One."* With your right hand lift the ball about eight inches by moving your wrist up. Put the napkin into your left hand again at *"Two"* and raise it again. At the count of *"Three"* snap your right wrist back, letting go of the napkin. It will fly back over his head. Your right hand drops into the left, which is then quickly closed. Open the left hand again, and the spectator will see that the napkin has vanished.

The fun part is in the fact that the rest of your audience will see where the napkin goes. The spectator does not and will be completely fooled. The tossed napkin will land silently, so your trick is foolproof.

Plates, Glasses, Cups, and Other Table Props

"A" IS FOR ASHTRAY

Several years ago I produced a magic show for the Society of American Magicians in New York. I booked an Italian magician named Delavagóne—whose unexpected stage name was Johnson. His comedy technique was exceptional, and the hit of his act was an adaptation of this table trick. He performed it on a large stage and used a small ashtray. The comedy came from the fact that no one in the audience was fooled. Like the Comedy Vanish with the napkin, only the victim—excuse me, the spectator—is fooled.

Your spectator is seated and you are standing next to him or her. You can use any small flat object, such as a butter dish or small plate, but I prefer a lightweight ashtray. Empty, of course.

The ashtray is held in your right hand with the thumb on the flat side, or bowl. *"We're going to play a little game with this ashtray."* Have him hold his hands palm up in his lap. *"Get ready to catch this when I drop it."* Move your arm up and bring it down toward his palms as you count, *"One,"* and touch his palm with the ashtray at the count *"Two."* Move the arm up and bring it down to his palm again. The third time, the arm goes up and you deposit the ashtray on your head. The arm comes down empty as you say *"Three."* He will look up, surprised.

At that moment your right hand goes to your left armpit as though you had just put something under your left arm. The arm snaps against the body. *"Where is it?"* Wait for his reply. *"Under my arm? Wrong."* Lift your right arm. *"The other side? Wrong again."* Turn your back to him and lift your right arm again. *"Oh, this arm. Wrong."* Then lift the left arm and show that there is nothing there either.

Point to the floor at his right. *"Look there."* As he turns to look, tilt your head and catch the ashtray with your right hand. Put it under your coat and bring it out as he turns to look at you. *"Here it is."* He thinks he caught you, so when you say, *"Shall we play again?"* he will probably accept.

"What's under there?" Point to his right. As he turns put the ashtray on your head again quickly. *"I got you again, it's gone."* Open both sides of your coat. *"It's under your chair."* He bends to look and you tilt your head, allowing the ashtray to fall. Catch it and put it in his lap. *"Wrong again."*

Take the ashtray and walk around behind him to the other side. You are out of his view for a split second, and you place the ashtray on your head again. *"Take it please."* Give him your empty palm. *"Up there."* Point upward. By this time he probably won't look up. Point your left index finger to the left just in front of his eyes. *"There!"* He must refocus, giving you time to tilt your head so that the ashtray falls into his lap. Look up toward the ceiling. *"Somebody up there likes you."*

The audience will have a lot of fun, and don't forget to thank the spectator for being a good sport. Above all, do not overdo this stunt. Too many vanishes make it boring.

"B" IS FOR BEER

Nothing dresses up a dinner table like an ice-cold glass of beer right from the tap. When I asked magician Lee Noble to show me his favorite table trick, he asked me to order a glass of light beer. *"What makes this trick your favorite?"* I asked. His reply: *"Because after I do this trick, I get to drink the beer."*

Pour a small bit of salt in a pile in front of you on the table. Place the cold beer glass, which is usually wet on the bottom, directly on top of the salt. *"I always like a bit of salt in my beer, but I never know just how much to add. I found that by using a bit of magic I get the right amount. Watch."*

Pick up the salt shaker and tap its bottom against the side of the beer glass. *"The right amount of salt will come up through the bottom of the glass."* The audience will see what appear to be grains of salt rising to the top of the glass— actually these are tiny white gas bubbles. Lift the glass and brush away the few grains of salt left on the table. The bottom of the wet glass will have picked up almost all of it. Be sure that you secretly wipe the salt from the bottom of your glass before tipping it toward the spectator as you drink the beer.

COFFEE MONEY

Optical illusions fool the eyes, and magical illusions fool the mind as well. This little miracle uses a bit of both, making it twice as effective.

You will need a cup and saucer. Remove the cup from the saucer and set it aside so that it is still within your reach. You will also need a package of paper book matches and a glass of water. There should only be about an inch and a half of water in the glass—about one quarter of its capacity. The amount of water used will affect the outcome of the trick.

"Let me show you how a magician makes some coffee money." Put your hands into your pockets as though looking for something. *"Do you have a nickel?"* As you are looking through the pockets, secretly take out a quarter and leave it in your lap, on your left leg near the knee.

Place the borrowed nickel in the center of the saucer. Now pull a match from your package. Bend the bottom of the match into a small L shape. Place this bent part under the coin so that the match is standing upright in the saucer —the weight of the coin will hold it in place.

Carefully pour all the water into the saucer, covering the coin. Make sure that the head of the match does not get wet. Light another match and touch it to the one in the plate. The moment that it ignites, invert the empty glass and cover the flame. Leave the glass in the saucer (Figure 45).

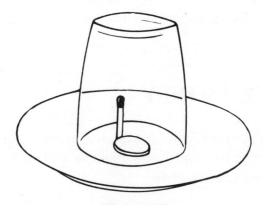

Figure 45

"Watch me make a profit." As the match burns, the water will rise and begin to move up inside of the glass. This will magnify the coin and you will get a perfect optical illusion. From the side, the spectator will see two coins in the plate, one larger than the other. *"Now we have two coins."*

While all eyes are on the water, casually drop the left hand to the lap and pick up the quarter. Hold it on the tips of your fingers. Your right hand lifts the saucer and places it in your left hand, covering the hidden coin. Your right hand moves to the top of the inverted glass. Turn the whole thing over very slowly, pouring the water into the empty coffee cup nearby. As the water begins to pour out, relax the pressure of your fingers on the outside of the plate and tip the glass a bit so both coins drop into the coffee cup.

Put your index finger into the cup and remove the coins, one coin at a time. *"Here is the nickel. And here is my profit. Almost enough for another cup of coffee. Who's buying?"* Show both coins on the table.

A DRY BET

Using the principle we just described, you can offer this variation as a bet. Place a dime in the saucer in front of you. Add enough water to cover the coin. You can bet that you will remove the coin without getting your finger wet.

To accomplish this stunt, tear a paper napkin so that you have about a quarter of it in your hand. Crumple it and drop it into an empty glass. Light a match to the paper so that it begins to burn. Invert the glass and place it alongside the coin. The flame burns up the oxygen in the glass, forming a partial vacuum. The water will rush into the glass, leaving the coin uncovered. Pull the dry coin out with your index finger.

MESMERIZED GLASS

Franz A. Mesmer was a German hypnotist who lived in the 1700's. He was one of the first scientists to use hypnotism in medical practice. Mesmerism, or hypnotism, was always considered allied to magic, since people could not explain how it worked. Hypnotists were thought of as either demons or magicians. But the last thing we want to do is put our audience to sleep. Instead let us entertain them with a demonstration of instant mesmerism, using a glass of water, a menu, and a cloth napkin.

"I am not a hypnotist, but I can perform a few simple experiments in mesmerism. May we try one?"

Pour some water into a glass so that it is about half full. With your right hand lift the glass and place it on the center of your menu, which is held in your left hand. Any flat surface will do as long as it can support the glass. Your left thumb is alongside the glass on the top of the menu with the rest of your fingers underneath.

"Please cover the glass with a napkin." A cloth dinner napkin is best, but if one is not available use a clean handkerchief. *"I will give you a few simple instructions. Please listen carefully. Lift the glass!"*

Your spectator can easily lift the glass through the napkin. *"Thank you. You may replace it, now that you are in my power. Remove the napkin, please."* The spectator does this, and you then add a little more water to the glass. *"Please cover the glass again."* Your right hand adjusts the top of the glass after it is covered. This gives you a chance to hold the glass while you do the next piece of business.

As soon as the glass is out of sight, bring your left index finger on top of the menu and grasp the glass between your index finger and thumb. The other fingers remain underneath the menu (Figure 46). Use your right hand to make a few mystical gestures in front of the spectator.

Figure 46. Note: Napkin not shown so that position of hand can be seen.

"Look into my eyes. You will try to lift the glass, but this time it will seem very heavy. You will not be able to lift it. Please try."

The spectator will be unable to move it. Let him or her try again with the other hand. *"Look into my eyes. You will now find it very easy to lift. Try."* Relax the tension of the index finger and the glass is easily moved. As the spectator does this, drop your left hand and toss the menu onto the table casually.

"What you have witnessed is basic mesmerism." Place your index fingers to your temples. *"I regret I cannot repeat it this evening; it is much too demanding."* All of this is said tongue in cheek. The audience will suspect that you used some scientific principle when you added the water. It was, in fact, merely an excuse for you to cover the method.

PROBLEM SOLVING

This is another cute table stunt, while we're on the subject of glasses. If you want to win something, call it a betcha. Here is our problem.

Three large wooden kitchen matches are placed under an inverted glass. A second glass is inverted next to it, and another kitchen match is wedged between the two glasses. (Small wooden matches do not always work.)

You can bet a beer that you can remove the three matches without allowing the wedged match to fall. Your friend cannot do it. (Unless he or she has already read this book, so check that first.)

The solution is really clever. The match is wedged between the glasses as described. The head is facing away from the glass with the matches underneath. Once the match is wedged so that it will not fall, ignite it with another match (Figure 47). As soon as the flame flares up, blow it out. This is

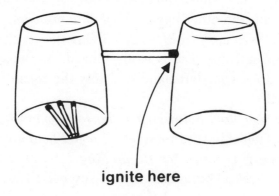

ignite here

Figure 47

important. Allow it to cool for a few moments—if it does not cool long enough it will fall. You can now lift the glass. The head of the match adheres to its side and will come along with it easily. Lift up the other glass and take the matches to win your bet.

ONLY ONE MOVE

There often comes a time in a restaurant when the conversation comes to a halt—the waiter has not returned with the dinner check, or perhaps the main course is delayed. This is the moment for a diversion. Keep your friends entertained with this problem.

Arrange six glasses in a single line on the table. Pour some wine or soda into the first three glasses on your left. The other three remain empty. Pose your problem. *"Can you move only one glass, so that the six glasses will be alternately full and empty?"*

Allow the spectators a few moments to try to figure this out. When they fail, show them how to accomplish the feat.

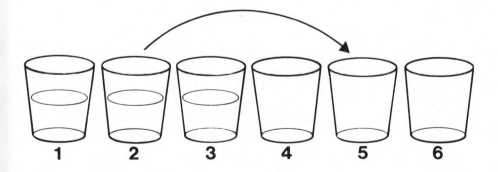

Figure 48

Lift glass number 2 and pour its contents into glass number 5 (Figure 48). You have moved only one glass by lifting it. The liquid is now in every other glass.

"*Without pouring the liquid into another glass, and with only one move, I will leave four glasses empty. Watch.*" Lift any of the wine glasses and drink the wine.

BOTTOMS UP

This is another "sucker effect." The sucker part is when the spectator thinks he catches you but ends up being wrong. Position three glasses so that they are in a line on the table. The center glass is inverted; the other two have their mouths up (Figure 49).

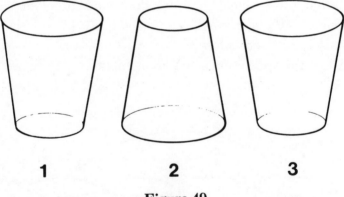

1   2   3

Figure 49

"*See if you can follow me. I will do this trick in three moves. I will move two glasses each time. I will make only three moves and will end up with all three glasses on the table* bottoms up." Do this once only, making the moves rapidly. Here is how to move the glasses.

First move: Turn glasses 2 and 3 upside down.
Second move: Turn glasses 1 and 2 upside down.
Third move: Turn glasses 2 and 3 upside down.

The glasses will end up as predicted, all bottoms up. Now here is the tricky part. Turn the center glass (2) up and offer to let the spectator try it. The secret lies in the fact that the spectator does not start with the glasses in the same position as you demonstrated it. Even if he has been able to follow your moves he will end up with the bottoms *down.*

"Let's both drink a toast to magic. Bottoms up."

NO PLACE LIKE HOME

Successful magicians perform their miracles by being careful to work under the proper conditions. You must always look your best, and every trick must work. Think before you start any procedure, making sure that you have the right props.

This trick requires a thin, worn-out dime. If you have only a new dime, do not attempt it. You will also need two shot glasses. One must be dry, the other still wet from a drink. If you have these requirements you can proceed.

Drop the dime on the table for all to see. *"This little guy is very unusual—he lives in a glass house. Like this one."* Set the dry glass on the table in front of you. Drop the dime into the glass. Shake it so that the audience will hear it jingle inside, and then pour the dime into the wet glass. The dry glass goes back to the table, mouth up.

"The little guy hates to leave home. One night I took him out to dinner." Turn your right palm up, taking the wet glass between the thumb and index finger. Turn the glass slowly, mouth down, on your left palm. The fingers of the left hand

close as you pretend to take the coin. It will actually adhere to the wet bottom inside the glass. Move your closed left hand farther to the left for misdirection. While the eyes follow that move, the right hand places its glass, mouth down, on top of the one on the table. Pick up both glasses together, holding them between the thumb and fingers (Figure 50).

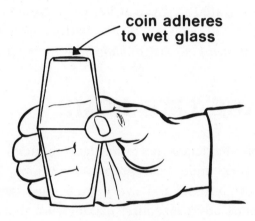

coin adheres to wet glass

Figure 50

"The dime was uncomfortable away from home. So he flew back." As you say this, make a throwing motion with the left hand toward the right hand. A shake of the right wrist causes the coin to dislodge. You will hear it drop into the bottom glass. Pour it onto the table. *"I'll have to fly home too. Will you pay the check to save some time?"*

BALANCING GLASS

If your hostess is using her best dinnerware and her fanciest stem glasses, this stunt is much more fun. Make it appear as though you are having a bit of difficulty at first, so that when the trick is accomplished it will be more effective. A sigh of relief will accompany the end of this feat—it will come from your hostess.

Use a large dinner plate or flat salad plate. Pick up the plate with your right hand. The bottom should be under your thumb while your four fingers hold the front of the plate. Turn the dish on its side so that the back of your hand is facing the audience. Pick up a glass. The fancier the glass the better, and a little wine or liquid in it makes it even more colorful.

Place the bottom of the glass on the edge of the plate. Adjust it this way and that way as if looking for the proper

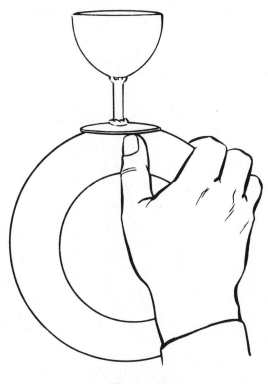

Figure 51

spot. Lift the glass and set it on the plate again. This time the front edge of the glass touches the edge of the plate. The rest of the glass extends over the back of the dish. Pull your right thumb back away from the plate without letting go. The base of the thumb does not move, only the first joint. The rear edge of the glass is now resting on your thumb tip (Figure 51).

From the audience's view the glass appears to be balanced on the edge of the plate. Remove the glass with your left hand. The right hand sets the plate on the table again.

Here is a variation of this stunt, done with an ordinary glass and a credit card. Take a credit card from your pocket or borrow one. You hold the card by its widest edge, thumb on one side, three fingers on the other. Balance the glass on

Figure 52

the narrow edge of the card, using your index finger to support it. It is a perfect illusion (Figure 52).

"I always use my credit card when I want to float a loan. Also when I want to float a glass."

FREEZE IT

Before you start this trick, secretly remove the clear cellophane from a cigar. Crumple the plastic into a small ball and have it handy in your lap or under your dinner napkin. When you're ready to begin place a glass of water in front of you on the table. The crumpled ball now is hidden in your hand behind the napkin. Lift your napkin and drape it over the glass. As soon as the glass is out of sight, drop the cellophane into the water.

"We'll just stir this up a bit." Pick up a teaspoon and bring it under the napkin, pushing it deeper into the water. The cellophane will open or expand. Remove the spoon and place your hand over the glass. Make a dramatic gesture and command the water. *"Freeze!"*

Gently lift the napkin. The glass will appear to have a large chunk of ice in the center. Hold it up in front of you, call the waiter, and hand him the glass. *"Would you please get rid of this, and bring me some water without ice."* Let the waiter get rid of the evidence. Everyone will know it's a gag, but don't explain it.

COOL IT

You have a piping-hot cup of coffee in front of you. You also have a loving spouse or a very good friend who will be your secret helper.

"There are several ways to cool a hot cup of coffee. You can stir it with a spoon, but that takes too long. You can put an ice cube in it, but that will dilute the coffee. Or you can use some magic. I prefer the last method. Watch."

Position the cup between you and your helper. Turn toward the cup and, spreading your fingers apart, hold your hand over the steaming cup. Draw the hand back to your body while closing the fingers. This is merely for effect. As the hand comes back over the cup again, open the fingers as before. By this time, all eyes are on the coffee. Your helper now takes a deep breath and surreptitiously blows on the steam coming up from the cup. The steam seems to disappear.

Don't drink the coffee—it's still too hot to handle.

THREE GUESSES

Tear a small piece from the corner of a paper napkin for this gag. Hand it to your dinner guest along with a pen or pencil.

"Please think of any number between one and a hundred and write it down." He does this. *"I don't want to see what you have written, so please fold the paper."* Take his folded paper and place it under your coffee cup. *"Allow me three guesses, and I will tell you what's on the paper."*

On the first try call out *"Number 37."* There is a very strong chance that this is the number he chooses. If you are correct, that is the end of the trick, and of course don't try to repeat it. If you are wrong take another guess: *"Number 35."* If you are still wrong you announce, *"This time I'm willing to bet anything that I will tell you what is on the paper. A cup of coffee is on the paper."* Lift up the cup and drink your coffee.

GLASS THROUGH HANDLE

"I will bet that I can push this drinking glass through the handle of this coffee cup." It seems impossible.

Here is the gag. Pick up a knife, pass it through the handle of the coffee cup and use it to push the glass. You are pushing the glass through the handle. You win the bet.

HATFUL OF WATER

This is one of the funniest tricks you can do at a party. It could even be presented on a stage or platform. The props can be made up in a matter of minutes. You will need two medium-size paper cups, the sturdy kind with a lip at the top. Prepare them beforehand, or in the privacy of the kitchen or washroom, neatly cut the bottom out of one cup. A sharp pocket knife will do, but a razor blade is better if you can find one. Carefully cut the top lip off the second cup (Figure 53). The bottomless cup (B) will then fit into the

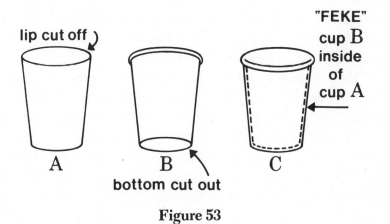

Figure 53

other cup (A). This is now what magicians call a *feke* (pronounced "fake"). It looks like a single cup.

Rejoin the party, find a pitcher of water, and get ready for some fun. This cannot be done if you are too close to your spectators. If possible the table you are working on should be higher than their eye level. You will borrow a hat and place it on the table, but the audience should not be able to see into the hat. In case they are too close, turn the brim up to block some of the view. Cup and pitcher are on your table. Set the hat in the middle of the table.

"I'm just learning magic, and here is a new trick from magic school that I must show you. Now this is the first time I've tried this, so you'll have to be a little patient with me. Is this a very expensive hat? It is? Good, I hate to use cheap props. Here is how the trick goes. We pour water into the hat. No, please don't get worried." Direct your patter to the owner of the hat. *"The cup goes into the hat."* Place the feke in the hat so that it stands up squarely in the middle. Keep your fingers in the cup. Now you separate the two parts inside the hat. This is easily done by pulling up with your index finger and pushing down with the thumb. Remove the insert (B), leaving the other half in the hat (Figure 54). Be careful that your audience doesn't see that the bottom is missing. If you lift the cup straight up and set it on the table, the bottom won't be seen. Make sure that the other part (A) is still standing upright in the hat.

"No, I seem to be wrong. The cup doesn't go into the hat." (This line is spoken as you remove the bottomless cup.) Stop and pretend to think for a while. *"The water goes into the cup, that's it."* Pick up the pitcher and pour some water into the feke in the middle of the hat. Not too much—it should be about half full.

"Oops! I forgot the cup." Put down the pitcher. Pick up

the bottomless cup (B) and carefully put it back into the hat. You are actually putting it back into the feke. By this time the laughter is building. Look at the owner of the hat. *"Please don't worry, I just fixed it. There's a cup in the hat. That will take care of the water."*

Look into the hat and do a double take. Pretend that something went wrong. *"Would you rather see a card trick?"* Reach into the hat, remove the feke cups, and pour the water back into the pitcher with a flourish. *"I'll do this trick again sometime, after I've perfected it."*

Crumple the cups and throw them away so that nobody can discover the secret.

Figure 54

2

Mind Reading
and ESP

Mentalism

Magic of the mind is a relatively new branch of our ancient art. Only in the past few hundred years have magicians done tricks involving the power of the mind. When presenting this type of magic you can appear to be serious, and you will find that most people want to believe that what you are doing is actually a form of mind reading, or telepathy.

To take advantage of this, your presentation is most effective when the patter is logical and the explanations sound scientific. The presentation is almost more important than the mechanics of the trick. You will find that the stunts are generally simple in nature and yet most startling and believable.

Remember that your purpose is to entertain, and you don't want to be thought of as a charlatan. Never represent yourself as a psychic or mind reader.

TELEPATHIC SENSITIVITY

Since you are going to experiment with mentalism you should know a few key words and definitions used by the parapsychologist (one who studies supernatural or extrasensory phenomena). The most popular tests used by mentalists are those involving telepathy. In telepathy, commonly called mind reading, thoughts are transferred from one mind to another.

For this test you should be seated at the table with people you know. Do not try this with children or members of your own family. *"Some years ago Duke University set up a study of telepathy and extrasensory perception. They wanted to determine if it was possible for one person to send a simple thought to another—if there was, in fact, a sixth sense. If two minds were in rapport with one another it might be possible for thoughts to travel. Let's try a simple experiment and hope that we are successful."*

Turn to one of your spectators. *"Please open your right hand and hold it palm up. Spread your fingers widely apart. I will ask you to concentrate on one finger. Your part in this test is extremely important. If you try to mislead me you will succeed, but if you really concentrate you can actually send a thought. Mentally try to tell me which finger you are thinking of."*

Touch your right index finger lightly to the tip of each of the spectator's fingers, one at a time. One finger will feel a bit different—it will offer a bit more resistance to your slight pressure than the others. When you get the feel of each of his fingers, you can name the one he has in mind.

This involves a subconscious physical reaction created by your spectator. If he is really trying to cooperate you will get the feel very quickly. Practice this, and it should not take too long to get the knack of it. Once you do, you will be successful most of the time. Don't give up if you fail at first.

This is a sensational opening for any mental effects that will follow. Since this is just a "test" you always have an out if it does not work the first time. Try a second person. You should succeed, and when you do, use this person as the subject for your next mystery. *"I believe you have paranormal sensitivity. May we try another experiment?"*

Work on this one until you get the right feel, and you will really astound people.

OUT OF SIGHT

This is another "test" of your telepathic ability. In this case you will suggest that you be blindfolded during the experiment *"so that I can concentrate without outside distraction."* Use a cloth dinner napkin or a pocket handkerchief for your blindfold. The other secret ingredient you will need is a confederate: your spouse or good friend.

Set a group of table objects in front of you on the table. These should all be within reach of your outstretched arm. Coffee cup, salt shaker, knife, spoon, dish, etc. Your helper should be seated either next to you or directly across the table. His foot must secretly touch yours.

"Sometimes it is easier to perceive thoughts emanating from more than one person at a time. So I will ask that for this test we all concentrate on the same object. I will blindfold myself so that I cannot see which object you choose. This will also help me avoid any distraction from the outside."

Either tie the blindfold yourself or have someone help you. If a blindfold is not available, turn your back or close your eyes.

"If you will please choose one object and tell me when you have done so, I will attempt to find the object by extrasensory perception. Now will everyone please concentrate."

When they tell you they are ready, move your hand around in front of you slowly. As soon as it is directly over the object, your helper will nudge your toe. At that point gently shake your wrist as though you were getting a vibration in the fingers. Bring your hand down on the object. *"I get a sudden feeling that this is what you selected."*

If you can identify the object by feeling it, name it. You can repeat this trick. It may be a good idea to pass the object at first and then come back over it for the second time before you name it. You will make it look a bit more difficult this way. The helper must be very much surprised and react as the others do.

Sometimes a skeptical onlooker will suggest that someone is helping you. Then you can say, *"You are all helping me by concentrating. If you do not concentrate I cannot succeed."*

MENTAL SPELLER

This is a variation of the Out of Sight trick, but it will require no outside help. It can be done with an audience as small as one and may be repeated, but not more than once.

You will need the following objects on the table: a cup, salt, plate, pepper, matches, teaspoon, cigarette, and tablespoon. Name each of the objects you will use, but not in the order just given.

"These are the objects that we will use for our test. Please concentrate on only one object. Do not tell anyone which one you have selected. Have you done this?"

Wait for a reply. *"Fine. In order for you to transmit this information I want you to spell the name of the object in your mind. Each time I tap your hand you will mentally spell one letter. As we come to the last letter you will please say stop. I will also ask that you close your eyes during this test so as to avoid distraction."*

For the benefit of the others at the table pass your hand over the various objects with your right index finger extended so you can point to each one. Each time you point to an object tap the spectator's hand once with your left hand. The first two times you will point to any objects. On the third try you will point to the cup, the fourth time to the salt, the fifth time to the plate. Each object is spelled with the same number of letters as the number of taps you are giving the spectator (Figure 55). You must, therefore, point to them in order. As soon as he calls "stop" your finger is pointing to the object he spelled to. Lift the object and instruct the spectator to open his eyes. *"Is this the one you chose?"*

Object	Number of Letters
Cup	3
Salt	4
Plate	5
Pepper	6
Matches	7
Teaspoon	8
Cigarette	9
Tablespoon	10

Figure 55

MONEY MENTAL

Later on we will deal with money magic, but since this unusual experiment involves mentalism we will use it here. Once again you will need a confederate. This time the method of communication is very subtle. You will need an empty coffee cup and a clear area in the center of your table, within reach of your confederate.

"This demonstration does not prove the existence of ESP

but merely serves to show you what can be done with mind control. Several minds together, concentrating on a single thought, can emit brain signals which I will attempt to interpret."

So far nothing has been done, but remember that the buildup is often more effective than the mechanics. You have set the stage for the test. *"When I turn my back I would like someone to place a single coin on the center of the table. Any coin will do."* Allow a minute for them to follow instructions. *"Is there a coin on the table?"* Wait for a reply. *"Fine. Will someone please use the coffee cup on the table to cover the coin so that it cannot be seen. I do not wish to see the money."*

Your confederate will be ready for your second instruction, and he or she will pick up the coffee cup and cover the coin. He will place it on the table so the handle will indicate to you the denomination of the coin, as shown in Figure 56.

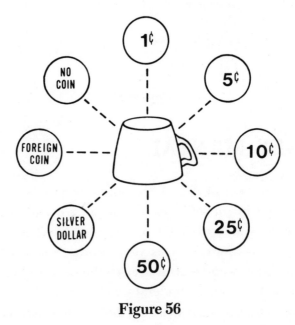

Figure 56

The cup will represent the center of a clock, with the bottom, or six o'clock, nearest the magician. The cup handle will represent the hour hand. Your helper, who has seen the value of the coin, will be able to set the cup handle pointing to the proper hour.

Three o'clock will represent a dime, six o'clock a half dollar, nine o'clock a foreign coin, etc. The spaces between those hours take care of the other coins.

There is always the outside chance that someone else will grab the cup before your assistant can get to it. That's nothing to worry about. Your helper merely lifts the cup to check the coin and sets it down again properly. He or she can comment, *"What is that coin again?"*

When all this has been done, you can turn back to the table. *"I am trying to get a clear impression. Will the owner of the coin please concentrate a bit harder."* At this point your helper gets busy again. He places his hands on the table in exactly the same position as the owner of the coin has his hands. In this way you can now tell whose coin was used. *"I am getting a strong impression now."* Point to the owner of the coin. *"It seems to be coming from here. Yours is a stronger signal. Is that your coin? It's a dime!"* (Name whatever coin was signaled.)

Should there be a foreign coin make it very impressive. *"I get the impression of the coin, but I cannot make out the value. It seems to be very strange—not an American coin. Am I correct?"*

In the event there is a wise guy who decides not to use a coin at all, you still come out on top. *"I'm sorry, but I am not getting any impressions. There is either some psychic interference or you are not concentrating hard enough. May we use another coin, please."* At that point your spectators will be sure that you have supernatural mental ability.

THOUGHT TRANSFERENCE

The sensational old vaudeville mind-reading acts always used two people. One person would sit on the stage blindfolded. The other would go into the audience holding up objects, and the medium on stage would name them. These tricks usually involved intricate codes and devices. For our dinner table we will use a simple two-person code that is quite versatile. We will assume that you have a friend, spouse, sister, or brother willing to work with you as your medium. Both of you must learn a few simple code words. We'll describe the code and then the method of using it. We will leave the presentation until last.

Study the chart in Figure 57. It is easy to memorize.

	Coins		Bills	
	Silent	*"Yes"*	*"Right"*	*"That's right."*
Silent	Penny	Quarter	$1	$20
"Yes"	Nickel	Half dollar	$5	$50
"Right"	Dime	Silver dollar	$10	$100

Figure 57

This is a money code. Your medium (receiver) will be able to tell a member of the audience which piece of money he or she is thinking about. The magician (sender), of course, must see the money so he can code it.

Reading from left to right on top of the chart, there are four divisions: two for coins and two for bills. As soon as he sees the money, the magician must picture the chart so he can see which column to use. Let us assume the money used here is a penny. This is in the first column of the coin section.

The medium always starts the trick by stating, *"You are thinking of a piece of money."* The magician remains silent so the medium knows that it is a coin and it is in the first column. He or she continues. *"I believe it is a coin."* The magician will again remain silent. This time, he is using the code on the left side of the chart. He has signaled the penny. The medium then names it: *"You are thinking of a penny."*

In that example no words were spoken by the magician. Now let us pick another coin. This time we'll use a half dollar. Watch what happens by following the chart and the dialogue.

Medium: *"You are thinking of a piece of money."*
Magician: *"Yes."* (Second column, top signal.)
Medium: *"I believe it is a coin."*
Magician: *"Yes."* (Left side, middle signal.)
Medium: *"You are thinking of a half dollar."*

Follow this example of a bill.
Medium: *"You are thinking of a piece of money."*
Magician: *"That's right!"*
Medium: *"I believe it is a bill."*
Magician: *"Yes."*
Medium: *"It is a fifty-dollar bill."*

Another example using the silent or no code.
Medium: *"You are thinking of a piece of money."*
Magician: *"That's right!"*
Medium: *"I believe it is a bill."*
Magician: (Remains silent.)
Medium: *"It is a twenty-dollar bill."*

By following the chart you can see how we arrive at any one of the coins and bills on the chart. In coming years the two-dollar bill may become popular again. Rather than make up a new code, just use a single word. After the first statement by the medium, simply say *"Correct,"* and both of you will know that a two-dollar bill was selected.

Should you want to expand this even further you can use *"That's correct"* as the code for foreign money. In this case the first statement would be:

"You are thinking of a piece of money."

"That's correct."

"I believe it is foreign."

"Right."

"It is a bill." (Etc.)

Here is a presentation you could use. *"Ladies and gentlemen, I am sure that you have noticed that a thought often occurs to two people at the same time. You start to say something, and your friend says the same thing at that exact moment. Many people might think nothing of this, or attribute it to coincidence. But we think there is more to it than chance. Two people close to one another often have minds that are in rapport—husbands and wives, very close friends, brothers and sisters, for example. My partner and I have found that our minds are tuned to each other's most intimate thoughts.*

"For this test I will blindfold my partner so that you cannot accuse us of using signals or gestures to communicate with one another." Do this. *"I will attempt to send thoughts directly to my partner without the use of the five normal senses. I would like someone to assist me, please, by giving me a piece of money, either a coin or a bill. I will hold this tightly in my hand so it cannot be seen."* Take a bill or coin bringing your hand to your forehead. Do not speak again.

The medium now goes into the act. Let us use another example here. The money is a dime.

Medium: *"You are thinking of a piece of money."*

Magician: (Remains silent.)

Medium: *I believe it is a coin."*

Magician: *"Right."*

Medium: *It is small, silver. I see a dime. Am I correct?"*

Magician: *"Wonderful. Shall we try once again?"*

Accept another piece of money and repeat the test. Do not do it for a third time—a bright spectator might catch on to your code.

Should you want to vary the test you can use table objects. The chart in Figure 58 shows how common objects can be coded, or you can make up your own.

	Silverware	Made of Glass	Dinnerware	Food
	Silent	*"Yes"*	*"Right"*	*"That's right"*
Silent	Spoon	Drinking glass	Cup	Bread
"Yes"	Fork	Salt shaker	Saucer	Celery stick
"Right"	Knife	Sugar bowl	Dinner plate	Olive

Figure 58

The dialogue might sound like this:

Medium: *"You are thinking of something on the table."*

Magician: *"Right."*

Medium: *"It is some kind of dinnerware."*

Magician: *"Yes."*

Medium: *"It is a saucer."*

Now that you have the idea you can make up your own charts for objects in your pockets, at home, or in the office. Have fun.

BRAINPOWER

As long as you have trained a medium whose mind is in tune with yours, the two of you might as well get together for other experiments. You can now vary your act the next time you have dinner with the same people. Here is another way to signal one another. In this case we will signal numbers. Send your medium out of the room, or blindfold him or her.

"The brain is as complex as any computer. It sends signals to many parts of the body. It sends thoughts to various body sensors. The fingertips are often good receivers of these unseen impulses. My assistant can pick up signals from my brain quite easily using only his [or her] sensitive fingertips. We will show you how this is done. Let us decide on a number: any number between one and 999. What number shall we use?"

If the medium is still in the room have the number written instead of called out. As an example we will use number 132. Ask someone to call the medium back into the room. You will be seated and the medium will stand directly behind you. The medium's middle fingertips gently touch each side of your head at the temples, just above and to the side of the eye line.

Your mouth is closed, teeth together. Grit your teeth, tightening your jaw. Now relax. Your receiver will feel a movement in your temples when you do this. You have just sent the signal for number one. (The first digit of the selected number.) Pause for a moment and do it again. This time tighten three times, one after the next. You have signaled the second digit. The last time you will signal twice. Your receiver's fingertips have felt each signal.

The medium reveals the number this way. *"I am receiving letters and numbers. I will try to isolate them. I now have a number. Number one hundred. No, I am sorry; there seems to be more. Thirty! No. The complete number is clear now—132. Am I correct?"*

This bit of stalling helps to make the show more interesting. The number was easy to determine, but to make it look like mind reading you cannot arrive at it too quickly.

Here are a few important points. When the digit is a *zero* you must signal ten times. While you are signaling relax and do not tighten too hard or you will distort your facial muscles and give the truth away. Practice a few times to get the knack.

SIXTH SENSE

In vaudeville a stooge is the guy who usually is the butt of the comic's joke—the one who gets the pie in the face. In magic or mind reading he is a most important member of the act. He plays the subordinate role in the activity, but without him there is no magic. Be nice to him—you need him again for this trick.

Arrange six table objects in a straight line. Use small objects such as a fork, spoon, salt, cup, and roll. As you set them on the table, count them. *"Let's use six objects. I'll put them in a row. One here, two here, three, four, five, six."* By doing this you are telling your confederate which number is assigned to each object.

Ask the spectators to agree to concentrate on a single

object while you close your eyes or leave the table. When you return, take a fast glance at the table in front of your helper. He or she will have the hand in a natural, relaxed position with a few fingers extended. Four fingers represent object four, two fingers represent object two, etc (Figure 59).

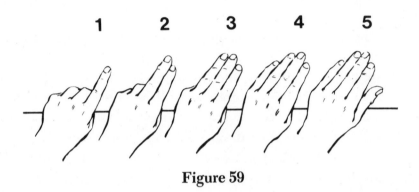

1   2   3   4   5

Figure 59

The number of fingers extended tells you which object was selected. If there is no hand on the table, it was number six.

As with other mental effects, take some time to come up with the answer and make the presentation very important and dramatic.

MAGICIAN'S CHOICE

Precognition is a beautiful word to play with when doing mental effects. It means the ability to foretell the future. The paranormalist (another great word) supposedly predicts happenings before they occur. The next group of tests will deal with predictions.

Before describing this first principle, I must take a moment to stress the importance of secrecy in the methods used in magic. I was reluctant to include the Magician's Choice principle in this book because professional magicians occasionally use it in earning their livelihood. The reason I succumbed is that I recently found it published elsewhere in a public work. I also have faith that you, being a responsible reader and interested in the art of magic, will not expose it.

What we are now dealing with is called a *force*. The mentalist makes sure that the outcome of his trick is what he predicted it would be. This force controls the events to follow.

Borrow three coins, each of a different denomination. Let us say that they are a penny, a dime, and a quarter. Lay them in a row on the table.

"You have three coins. I will take something of my own." Reach into your pocket and take out one coin—for example, a dime. It must be the same as one of the coins on the table. This will be your prediction. Your spectator is not to see the coin. It is held in your closed fist, which is placed in full view on the table near the other coins. The instructions to the spectator are important here. There are three possible outcomes.

"In my hand is a prediction of something that is going to happen." Lift the closed hand for a moment to emphasize this. *"Study the three coins on the table. Please pick up any two of these coins."*

1. If he leaves the dime on the table your trick is over. You will then say, *"You chose to leave the dime. You will notice that I predicted the dime."* Open your hand and take your bow.

2. Let's assume that he picks up the dime along with another coin. You will then continue to speak as though you hadn't finished giving him the instructions: *"And give me one of them."* If he gives you the dime, leave it in the open palm.

Open the other hand and state, *"You gave me the dime, as I predicted you would."*

3. If he keeps the dime, put the coin he gave you on the table and continue: *"Is there any reason why you chose to keep the dime? You will note that I predicted it."* Open your hand and show the dime.

No matter what choice the spectator makes you can force the outcome to match your prediction. This is because you set the conditions, and the spectator did not know what was going to take place. You will need this technique for the next trick.

CHOICE PREDICTION

In this effect you are going to make your prediction in writing, to show there is no chance that you used sleight of hand. Use a paper napkin or the back of the menu. You are going to predict one of the objects on the table. Pick one of the taller objects, such as a glass, bottle, salt shaker, etc. Let us assume that you will predict the glass. Write the prediction on the menu: *"You will choose the glass."*

Fold the paper or menu so that no one can see what you have written and put it in a prominent place or hand it to someone for safe keeping. *"I have just made a prediction of something that is going to happen shortly. Sometimes these messages come upon me suddenly, as this one just did. We will need five objects."*

Arrange five objects on the table directly in front of the spectator. Place them so that two tall objects are positioned second and fourth from each end. The glass should be closer to the spectator's right hand (Figure 60).

Now give him these instructions. *"Lift both hands above*

Figure 60. Note: This drawing represents the spectator's view.

the objects, please. Reach down and touch an article." The odds are in your favor that he will pick the glass, and your trick is over. Have him read the prediction. If he *does not* touch the glass, you must add, *"No, I meant touch an article with each hand."* Should one of the two articles now include the glass, you continue, *"Lift them please. Hand me one of them."* If he gives you the glass, say, *"Was there a reason why you gave me the glass?"* Have him read the prediction.

If he hands you the other object, say, *"You decided to keep the glass—just as I predicted. Please read the message."* If he had selected two other objects, casually set them aside. *"That leaves three items on the table."* You will then go on with the effect as you did with the three coins, treating the glass as you did the dime. Here is how you handle it.

"Three objects. Pick up any two." 1. He leaves the glass. *"Only the glass remains. That is what I predicted."* 2. He picks up the glass and another object. *"Hand me one of them."* 3. He gives you the glass. *"Of all the objects on the table you have chosen the glass. Please read my prediction."* 4. He keeps the glass. *"One chance in five. You have selected the glass. Please read my prediction."*

Never repeat any version of the Magician's Choice.

Pencil and Paper
Wizardry

A LITTLE PSYCHOLOGY

A few years ago my dear friend Frank Garcia and I produced a trick which we sold to the magic market. It was called Farky Hollis Predicts, a gag routine involving predictions and playing cards. It is based on the fact that the average person, one who does not work with math or magic every day, will make obvious responses to certain questions.

You probably know that if you ask someone, *"Quickly name a ferocious animal,"* he will probably say *"Lion."* If you give him an extra minute to think he might come up with *"Tiger."* If he must think quickly he offers the simplest reply. Using a little knowledge of psychology you can predict simple reactions.

Here is our test. On a paper napkin, menu, or business card write the number 37. Fold the paper so that no one can see what you have written. Place this under a glass for safekeeping. You are going to offer directions that will elicit a quick reply. Be very careful that the wording is exact and that your subject understands you.

"Please think of an odd *number between 1 and 50. Make* both *digits odd, but not exactly the same; not 11, for example. Are you thinking of such a number?"* The normal response to this is 37. A second possible choice is 35.

"Are you thinking of number 37?" If the answer is yes,

the trick is successful. If he should reply no, hand him your prediction and add, *"I was going to write number 35. What was your number?"* If he did not pick that alternate but came up with 19 or 17, you are still covered, since these *are* experiments which do not necessarily work all the time. You will be right more often than not.

If you think about how this works you will see that you gave your subject more restrictions than he realized. You have limited him to numbers between one and fifty that have odd digits: 1-3-5-7-9. You have eliminated any duplicates: 11 and 33. You have also subtly suggested that he think of numbers higher than 11. He heard 11 so he will think higher. The choices left to him are very few.

If you want to try the same thing with another person, change the rules a bit. *"Please think of an* even *number between 50 and 100. Make both digits even, but not exactly the same."* The number most often selected is 68. The second alternate is 86. While not 100 percent perfect, this will work often enough to earn you a reputation.

PSYCHOLOGICAL QUICKIES

Taking advantage of the spectator is easy when you know the normal answers to "quickie" questions. Here are a few stunts that are quite amazing to the uninformed.

1. Ask for a number between 1 and 9. The answer usually is 7.

2. Have your subject draw *"a simple geometrical figure such as a hexagon, square, or octagon."* Odds are that your spectator will draw a triangle.

3. *"Think of two geometrical shapes, with one drawn*

inside the other. Don't pick a square; that's too easy." Your spectator will most often draw a circle and a triangle.

4. Draw the letters A B C D E on a piece of paper. Request that the spectator circle one. It is usually the letter C—the one in the middle.

5. Place four similar-sized objects in front of the spectator. If he is right-handed he will pick the third from his left. The same thing applies to numbers. On one side of your business card write, *"Why do all nuts pick 3?"* Showing only the front of the card, boldly write the numbers 1 2 3 4. Ask that the spectator *"pick a number. What number is it?"* It is usually 3. Show him the other side of the card for a quick laugh.

Now you have the basis for some simple experiments. Try a few, but make predictions out of them. You can write on a single sheet of paper, *"During this experiment I predict someone will select number 3. Someone will draw a triangle and a circle. A third party will choose the letter C."* Fold the prediction and put it on the table.

Now start your test. Draw four numbers and allow one spectator to *"think of a number; do you have one in mind?"* Go to the second one with some paper. *"Think of two geometrical shapes. . . ."* Print A B C D E on a piece of paper for the third party. *"Please circle one letter."* (On this last one, in case they do not pick C you can fall back on the Magician's Choice and ensure at least one correct prediction.)

When you open the prediction slip your audience should be amazed: at least two out of three of your predictions should be correct. Pick the person who gave the right answer and use him for your next experiment. *"You have a good 'psychic interpretation'"* (whatever that means).

A SYMBOL TRICK

While on the subject of pencil and paper stunts, let us go back to a "telepathy" effect for a moment. Draw five ESP test symbols on a sheet of paper, as shown in Figure 61.

Figure 61

"These are the five designs used at Duke University when Dr. Rhine was conducting his experiments there some years ago. It was believed that the mind could transmit simple designs easier than complete thoughts. If you would all concentrate on one of these, perhaps I can get the impression."

Turn your back while one is being selected. Turn around again and name the design. How? Our old friend the confederate.

You can use either the hand-signal code for five objects or another simple one that is also natural-looking. The helper has a cigarette. If it is in his left hand the symbol was number 1. If it is in the left side of his mouth, number 2. The middle of his mouth represents the center of the paper, the right side number 4, and the right hand number 5.

You can see how easy it is to make up experiments, once you know the system. The use of the Zener ESP symbols makes the trick more interesting and puts it into the realm of mentalism.

PSYCHOTHESIA

When the conversation gets around to mentalism, ESP, or clairvoyance, get ready to discuss "psychothesia." Don't bother looking it up in the dictionary—it isn't there. We made it up just for this experiment. If you like word roots, it was taken from *aesthesia,* involving the sense of touch, and *psycho,* which involves the processes of the mind. And while we're on words, you may have noticed that we refer to these tricks as "experiments." Experiments sound a lot more like science than like trickery.

In this experiment you will need a few pencils, some paper, and nine spectators. It can be done at the dinner table or on a stage in a theater. A sheet of paper is best for the trick, but if none is available use a paper napkin. Tear the napkin into nine equal pieces as shown in Figure 62. Tear the pieces neatly and slowly. You will note that in doing this

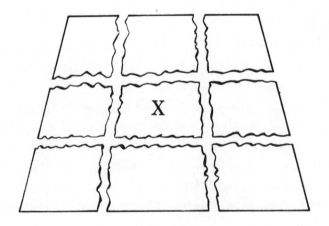

Figure 62

you will have one piece in the center (X) that has four ragged edges. All the other pieces will have at least one straight edge. Keep track of this piece (X) to see who gets it. That person is your "key" spectator.

"In recent years scientists have been experimenting with various kinds of mental phenomena. Telepathy, ESP, and the other remarkable powers of the human mind are still mysteries to us." Patter as you tear the sheets carefully.

"One such subject is psychothesia. It is thought that the brain emits minute electrical impulses during the thinking process. These impulses are often picked up by another person's brain. Since the various languages are not the same, the receiver is unable to translate the signals. But his senses are often affected by the emissions." Spread the papers around on the table, mixing them a bit but keeping track of the key piece.

"If each of you will take a piece of paper, I'll try an experiment that you might enjoy." Watch to see who picks up the key. Point to him or her. *"I'll hand you a pencil, and I would appreciate it if you would write the name of some woman, living or dead. Please write only the first name, and do not let anyone see what you are writing."* Hand him or her a pencil. If other pencils are available give them to the other spectators. *"The rest of you will please write a man's name. Any man, living or dead. Only write the first name."*

As they are busy doing that you obtain an empty soup bowl or coffee cup. *"Please fold the papers once, and then once again the other way."* Ask one person to collect the slips. *"I do not wish to touch them as yet."*

Instruct the collector to deposit all the slips in the bowl or cup.

"Now I will ask you ladies and gentlemen to cooperate with me in the following way. Will the person who wrote

down the woman's name please raise your hand. Thank you. Will you please concentrate deeply on the name that you wrote. The others please do not concentrate at all. Merely watch. Thank you."

Dip into the bowl and remove the papers one by one, holding each of them to your forehead and giving each serious thought. Place each one on the table as you are apparently through with it. You are really examining them to see if the edges are straight or torn. The one with all the edges ragged is your key. As soon as you find it, pause.

"Does the letter M mean anything to anyone present?"

You might get an answer. If it is from one of the other spectators you say, *"I asked you not to concentrate. Please!"* If the key spectator replies, you have a striking miracle. No matter what the reply, you ask, *"What is the name you wrote, please?"* Hand the slip to any other spectator. *"Please read the name on the paper. It is a lady's name. A combination of the sense of touch and the remarkable processes of the mind. One name singled out of many. Psychothesia."*

To vary the effect you can select one odd number in a group of even numbers, the name of a dead person among a group of living names, etc. Try not to make this one seem like a game, but more of a mental experiment.

WRISTWATCH PREDICTION

Each Saturday in New York City a small group of six or seven gentlemen meets in a midtown office building to discuss mentalism and mind reading. A few are professional mentalists and others just magic buffs who love the art. They discuss ways of performing various effects, and it is always a treat to hear of their discoveries. One member of this group is a very close friend of mine named Lee Noble. Lee is a professional entertainer. Although the origin of this trick is unknown to me, I do know that I first saw Lee Noble perform it in 1965. The effect is astounding, the method is bold, and it will certainly be talked about for a long time after you do it.

In this instance I will describe the effect of the trick before explaining how to accomplish it. You will write a prediction on a piece of paper and put it in a prominent place. No one can touch it. You now ask any spectator to lend you his or her wristwatch. You wrap this in a cloth napkin, making a pocket by putting all four ends together.

Your spectator is asked to call any one of the waiters near your table. You now instruct the waiter to take the watch into the kitchen or out of your sight and turn the stem so that the time is changed. He is then to bring the watch back.

He returns with the watch set at a new time. The prediction is read, and the time exactly matches the prediction. Any waiter, any restaurant, any watch with a winding stem can be used in this miraculous experiment. Here is how it is done.

You will need to prepare for this trick by folding a dollar bill into a small package about an inch square. You will also need a small piece of paper, which you can make from one of your business cards. One third of the card is enough. Print the following on the card:

> This is a gag. Please help me
> by setting this watch at 5:10.
> Keep the bill for your trouble.
> Thanks for keeping this a secret.

If you have a paper clip, attach the note to the bill. This package is small enough to fit into your palm, and don't make any special covert move to hide it. Be natural. You can keep it in your lap or coat pocket until you need it.

Borrow a pencil and some paper and write your prediction. *"A borrowed watch will be set to read 5:10 exactly."* Fold the prediction and hand it to someone to put in an obvious place. Under a glass in the center of the table is fine.

"I have just written a prediction of a coming event that just occurred to me. I would like your permission to test this strange feeling I just had. Will someone lend me a wristwatch or pocket watch? Something that we can see easily. Thank you." Examine the watch and show it around. Pull the stem to change the setting. *"This setting can be changed easily. Can we have a napkin, please."* Place the napkin on the table. Set the watch aside and make a small bag by folding the napkin. The left hand holds all the ends and you have a pocket. This resembles the Utility Napkin trick we described earlier.

Your right hand goes into your pocket or drops to your lap to pick up the bill and note. *"Where is the watch?"* Place your right hand in the pocket formed in the napkin. It goes into the section closest to you. Leave the note there. *"I have just made a bag. The watch will be safe here."* Pick up the watch and put it into the napkin bag at the pocket farthest away from you. Do not try the middle, there is nothing there to hold it.

"So that you do not think I have planned this or that I gave special instructions to anyone, please call any waiter or busboy to the table." (Getting a waiter may be the hardest part of the trick.) Once he has arrived you hand him the napkin. *"Waiter, I wonder if you would help us. There is a watch wrapped in this napkin. We're trying an experiment. Would you take this watch out to the kitchen or any place*

where you cannot see us. Spin the stem on the watch so that the time is changed. Just turn it at random a few times and bring it back to us. Thank you."

Your waiter will look very surprised—this is not his everyday fare. When he gets your note, you can be pretty sure that the dollar will influence him and he'll follow instructions. He will also wait around to see what has happened, enjoying the knowledge that he played a part in your gag.

Have the prediction read before revealing the time on the watch. And make sure that you don't touch the watch when it is returned to the table. You wouldn't want to be accused of hanky-panky. The effect will cost a dollar, but it will be one well spent.

PAST AND PRESENT PRESIDENTS

After a few dinner parties you will find yourself deluged with requests for some of your amazing predictions. This one is very easy to perform impromptu.

Pick up your menu and boldly write the name "Lincoln." Cover the prediction with a plate so that no one can see what you have written.

"Will you, sir, give me the name of any one of our past or present presidents, living or dead." This can almost be considered a psychological force. The most commonly named president is Lincoln. If your spectator names Lincoln right off, you have a great success, so build up the drama.

"You chose the name Lincoln by yourself. I did not arrange this with you beforehand, did I? This was a free choice. Please lift the plate and read my prediction."

Let us suppose that he named a different president:

"*Washington.*" At this point pick up a pad or one of several pieces of paper napkin you'll have ready. Write the word "Lincoln" as you speak the name "Washington." Fold the paper and drop it into a coffee cup or deep dish. "*May we have another president, please.*" As each name is called you write "Lincoln" but say the name of the president they select. "*Ford, like the car.*" Always fold each paper and put it into the dish.

Someone will finally name Lincoln. Put the paper on the table as you write so that your neighbor can see you actually writing the name. Make a big flourish of dotting the *i*. "*That should be enough; we have five or six different names to work with.*" Empty the bowl on the table and spread the names. Ask that some of the spectators hand you the folded slips one at a time, until only one paper is left on the table.

"*One name remains. I will give you an option. Either leave that name or take one of mine in exchange.*" No matter which course they follow, there will be a "Lincoln" slip on the table.

"*The odds are one in six that I am correct. Read the paper please.*" Pause for the reply. "*Lincoln? Read my prediction.*"

This leaves you with the incriminating evidence in the palm of your hand. Casually crumple the papers and drop them into your pocket.

KEEP AHEAD

The method used for this demonstration is called the *one-ahead system*. This principle keeps you one jump ahead of your onlookers. Use a paper pad if one is available. If not, a paper napkin can be torn to give you a few slips of prediction paper.

"*I can feel that you are a mentally receptive group, and*

I'd like to demonstrate three types of mental phenomena. I will try to show you clairvoyance, telepathy, and precognition at work."

Point to any spectator. *"Do you know how much change you have in your pocket right now? Just answer 'yes' or 'no.' You're not sure? If you don't know how much there is, I certainly cannot know either. This will be a test of clairvoyance."*

Take a square of paper and write the word "Dime" on it. Fold the paper in half and then in half again the other way, so that no one can see what you've written. On the outside of the paper you will write the number 3. As you do this you must patter, *"We will call this test number 1."* Drop the paper into a coffee cup with the number side down so it is not seen.

"Will you please go into your pocket and remove all the loose change. Drop the coins on the table so we can all count it." Let us assume it totals $1.18. You will remember this amount. Hand a sheet of paper to another person nearby. *"Will you be the recordkeeper? Please write the number 1 and the amount of $1.18 next to it. Thank you."*

Look for a dime among the coins. If there is one, set it aside with two other coins of different value. If there is no dime, let him put the money away. You will use your own later.

"Now I would like to try some telepathy." Ask another subject to arrange four or five small objects on the table. He or she is to concentrate on any one of the items. *"Do not tell anyone what you are thinking of until we ask."* Pretend to be getting a mental impression. Pick up another slip of paper and write $1.18. Fold the paper again and write a number on the outside. *"This is test number 2."* You actually write number 1 on the paper. Drop it into the cup with the first slip. *"Now you may tell us what you selected. The cigarette?"*

Direct the recordkeeper. *"At number 2, please write 'Ciga-rette' "* (*or whichever item was named*).

"My last test will be a prediction. I will write this first and then give you instructions." Write the word "Cigarette" and after folding the paper put a number 2 on the outside. *"This is test number 3."* If there were three coins left on the table, use them. If not, reach into your pocket and bring out three coins, one of them being a dime. The last spectator will choose the dime by means of the Magician's Choice.

"Recordkeeper, test number 3 is complete. Please write down a dime. If you will now read the results of the experiment we will see how we did." Turn the cup upside down after shaking it a bit, so that all the papers fall out at random. Allow the papers to be opened and check them against the list. Every prediction is correct.

MAGIC WITH NUMBERS

Magicians have always used the sciences to create their mysteries. There are chemical tricks, effects involving the principles of physics, and many using the curiosities of optics. Mathematics can play an important part in im-promptu magic. If you enjoy doing mind-reading tricks you will find that your knowledge of arithmetic will be very important to you.

While I was researching this book one name kept coming up. Martin Gardner, mathematician and writer, is the undisputed king of magical math tricks. Mr. Gardner has collected, invented and catalogued impromptu tricks for many years, and his love for magic helped us all. On behalf of all magicians I take it upon myself to thank him here.

THE NUMBER NINE

One of the sessions at the School for Magicians in New York is described as "mental night." In this lesson we teach many of the basic principles of mind reading, such as the psychological force and the one-ahead principle. The most fascinating tricks of the evening are those using the *nine principle*. One young math teacher taking the course spent an entire day working out the equations of why this works. I shall leave it to the mathematicians to worry about that. Here is what we can do with it.

Write down any number containing three different digits. Reverse the digits and you have a new number. Write the smaller number under the larger number so that you can subtract one from the other. The result is another new number. Reverse the digits of the result and add the two numbers together. Your total is 1089. Yes, it always works.

Example: Original number 743

```
    743
  −347    (Reversed)
    396    (Result of subtraction)
  +693    (Reversed)
  1089    (Total)
```

Study the result of the first subtraction. The center digit is always 9. The two outer digits will total 9. Add all the digits together and they total 18. If there are two digits in the result it will be 99 and these digits also total 18. Add the 1 + 8 and you get 9 again.

A	B	C
3 9 6	3 9 6	3 + 9 + 6 = 18
(Center digit 9)	(Outer digits total 9)	

Let's use the principle in a prediction effect. Write the number 1089 on a sheet of paper or napkin. Write the last digit so that it looks like an upside-down 6. Fold the prediction and set it on the table under an ashtray. Give your spectators the instructions we used above for the original subtraction and addition. *"Have you a final total?"* (Pause.) *"Do I see four digits?"* °

Wait for his reply, then open the prediction paper. Open it upside down so that the result looks like 6801. Announce the prediction: *"6801."* Wait for the response, then pretend to catch your mistake. *"Oh, I'm sorry. The paper is upside down. 1089."*

MENU COUNTDOWN

Using our knowledge of the "nine principle" we can create many new tricks. Mathematical tricks can be used for mind reading or telepathy effects. The same trick can be treated as a prediction if you prefer.

This one involves the dinner menu. Count down to the eighteenth item on the menu and remember the name of the dish. Let us assume, for example, that it reads "Roast Beef." Here is how to have some fun.

Study the menu. *"I never know which dish to pick, so I invented a game that selects the food for me by chance. Will*

° There is an outside chance that the result will be 198. If the spectator replies *"No"* to your four digits question, you then read the prediction as 198. Crumple the paper and put it in your pocket without showing it.

you help me choose?" Hand the spectator the menu. He can write on the back.

"Please write down any three-digit number you like—just make sure all the digits are different." Wait for him to do this. *"If you reverse the digits you have another number. Do this so we have two random numbers to work with."* Wait a moment for him. *"Please subtract the smaller number from the larger number. And I hope you're good at this because I really like roast beef. Have you got an answer yet?"* Wait again. *"Good. I can practically taste that rare roast beef. Add up all the digits in the total. What did you get? Eighteen. Fine. Open the menu and count down eighteen items. What did we finally choose? Roast beef? Boy, am I glad you're having dinner with me."*

The result, of course, had to be eighteen.

MENU TELEPATHY

This is a variation of the previous trick that will look like real telepathy, even to skeptics. Should they try their own numbers when you're not looking, they will get a different result. Decide on a section of the menu to use. We will assume you pick the entree section, which usually has the largest number of choices. You need at least nine dishes.

Choose two people sitting next to each other as your subjects. Casually make sure that each has a menu exactly like yours—sometimes there are variations that could be fatal to your trick.

"I'd like to try an experiment in mental telepathy. Please use the back of your menu." Point to the first spectator. *"Write down any number having three digits, all different. Do not show it to me. Merely pass it to your neighbor."*

Now instruct the neighbor, *"Will you please reverse the digits of the number you see written. This will give you a new number. Write the new number. I cannot possibly know what numbers are written there. Let us make it more impossible. Please subtract the smaller number from the larger number so that you have a new total chosen completely at random."* Wait until this has been done. *"May I assume your result is also a three-digit number?"* The odds are that he will say it is; if not, the result is 99, and we will deal with this later.

"Please open your menus and look at the entree section. There seems to be a large selection there. I will instruct you to select an item based on the numbers you arrived at. For example, what was the first digit of your result?" Let's say, for example, that he tells you the digit was 6. You now know several things. First, that the middle digit is 9, because it always is. Second, if you subtract the first digit from 9, the answer is the last digit. Since the first is 6, you know that the last digit is 3.

Open your menu to give them further instructions. *"Your digit is 6, so you will count to the sixth item and remember it."* As you close your menu you get a quick look at items 9 and 3. Remember these as your instruct them further. Point to the first subject. *"Will you look up the dish represented by the second digit?"* To the second say, *"And you please remember the item represented by the last digit. Do not tell me which choices you both have made, merely concentrate upon them."*

Finish the trick by either revealing the dishes letter by letter as you would a word. Or you might describe the dish making it interesting. *"I can see a baked potato sitting on the side of the plate. . ."* etc.

Should the answer have been 99, which is a possibility,

you do not ask for the first digit, merely explain what you want done while you are looking at the menu and remember the ninth dish. Since they are both concentrating on the same item you can make it more interesting. After revealing the first subject's choice, tell the second subject, *"You seem to be concentrating on the first dish; please think only of your own. I seem to be getting the same thought twice. Did you choose the same dish, by chance?"*

The results of the subtraction will always be one of the numbers in the illustration, or 99.

198	594
297	693
396	792
495	891

THE MISSING NUMBER

Write any number and add all the digits together. If the result is more than one digit, add those together until you are left with a single numeral. This number is the digital root of the original number.

Example:	Original number	9578
	Add digits	$9 + 5 + 7 + 8 = 29$
	Add	$2 + 9 = 11$
	Add	$1 + 1 = 2$
	Digital Root of	$9578 = 2$

Any number may be scrambled by using the same numerals to form another number. Subtract one from the other, and your answer will always have a digital root of 9.

Here is how to use this principle in a test of "telepathy." Give the spectator the following instructions:

"Write down any number you like. It may have three, four, or five digits, or more if you like arithmetic." Wait for him to do this. *"Use the same numerals, only this time scramble them to form another number. When you have this, subtract the smaller number from the larger number."* Wait again. *"We now have a result that was chosen entirely at random. There is no way anyone could have predicted in advance what that number is. Please circle a single digit in it. Do not let me see what you are doing. Tell me when you have done this.*

"Concentrate on the digit you circled. Concentrate harder—I seem to be getting too many numerals. Call off the numerals that remain, crossing them out as you do this. In this way you will clear your mind. Call them in any order you like."

As he is calling out the numerals, you are mentally adding them in your head. Once you have a total, add those digits until you are left with a single root number. Subtract the root from 9 and you have the digit he circled. In the event that he circled a 9, the root you come up with will also be 9.

Example	His selection	98654
	Scrambled	86459
	Subtracted	12195
	Selection #2	1 ② 195
	Add remainder	1 + 1 + 9 + 5 = 16
	Add	1 + 6 = 7
	Subtract from 9	9 − 7 = 2

"The digit you circled is a two!"

Should you wish to repeat the effect, have him write another number. This time he is to add all the digits to give him a second number. He subtracts again and his total will have a root number of 9. Repeat the steps described above.

A PENNY FOR YOUR THOUGHT

There are so many possibilities for tricks using one or another variation of the nine principle that you will find yourself making them up on the spur of the moment. Here is a coin stunt that works with a "nine" force.

Drop ten pennies into a saucer on the table. Offer your spectator a pencil and paper. *"I will turn my back, and we will arrive at a random number by some simple arithmetic. Please write any three-digit number. Make all the digits different. Now reverse the digits so that you have a new number."* Wait for him or her to do this. *"Add the two numbers. Now add the digits in that total so that you are left with a single numeral. Have you got that?"* Wait for a reply.

"Now please remove as many pennies from the dish as is indicated by your total. For example, if your total is 6 take away six cents. If the total is 3 take away three pennies. Do this quietly so I cannot count the coins as you remove them." Wait for a few moments.

"Cover the remaining coins with a napkin or coffee cup so I cannot see how many there are as I turn around." Turn back to the table and put your hand over the covered saucer. Concentrate and gesture a few times to make some magic and then announce, *"There is a single penny left. A penny for your thought."*

The total is 9—he will always get this root number. The patter leads the spectator astray. He will come away believing that it may have been possible for him to have selected a 3 or 6 total. Do not, of course, repeat this trick, because the amount is always the same.

MULTIPLYING FUN

This is an unusual stunt that your guests will enjoy playing with, although there is no magic involved. It is another one of the amazing things you can do with the number nine.

Jot down eight digits from 1 through 9 *omitting* numeral 8.

$$1\ 2\ 3\ 4\ 5\ 6\ 7\ 9$$

Ask your spectator to circle any one of the digits. Now you give him another number, which he will multiply by the original number. His result is a total consisting of an entire series of the digit he circled.

Watch it work. The number you will give him is his own digit multiplied by 9. For example, if he circles number 3 you mentally multiply this by 9, which gives you 27. This is written under the series, and you hand him a pencil for his work.

$$
\begin{array}{r}
1\ 2\ 3\ 4\ 5\ 6\ 7\ 9 \\
\times\ 2\ 7 \\
\hline
8\ 6\ 4\ 1\ 9\ 7\ 5\ 3 \\
2\ 4\ 6\ 9\ 1\ 3\ 5\ 8 \\
\hline
3\ 3\ 3\ 3\ 3\ 3\ 3\ 3 \\
\end{array}
$$

If you have a pocket calculator in your briefcase it's fun to watch the total light up.

AGE-OLD PREDICTION

You probably did a version of this trick when you were just a kid. The nice thing about doing magic is that it reminds you that you are really still a kid. You will write a prediction and as you usually do, put it on the table, and cover it. Hand your subject a pencil and paper and ask him to get busy.

"Please write down the year of your birth. I won't see it, so don't worry about giving your age away. Now directly under that, write down the year of some great event in history. It can even be the year of your marriage, or any date that is memorable to you. Let's see now, we need some more numbers. Add the number of people here at the table. Oh, yes, getting back to that date in history—how many years ago was that? Don't tell me, just write it down. Throw in today's date—not the year, just the day of the month. Now the big question: how old are you as of the end of this year? Write it—no one will see it, I promise. That's a big number you're writing. I think we have enough. Please add all the numbers until you have one final total." Wait until this is done.

"To protect the secret information, just tear off the part with the total and you can destroy the rest. Swallow it if you feel that it will be safer. What is your total? Please read my prediction. It matches."

The prediction you have written is twice this year's date, plus the number of the people at the table, plus the day of the month. When you asked for the first two dates plus the number of years ago they happened, the total would be twice this year's date. That is quite obvious. So we added a few extra numbers to throw the spectator off. We also did not follow any special sequence. In other words, we didn't ask for the year of birth and then the age. We separated these to keep the numbers apart and help confuse the spectators. Adding the extra numbers makes it harder for him or her to follow. You can add any numbers that you know, such as the score of a game, the number of your house, etc.

RAPID CALCULATOR

You can do this one by yourself, but it would be a nice gesture to use your secret confederate so that he or she can take a bow for once. Just remember not to do it at the same sitting that you are using a stooge trick. Your partner has paper and a pencil. You have another piece of paper and two spectators. Approach the first person.

"My partner here has a unique ability to calculate numbers at lightning speed. Let's try a test. Please write down any four-digit number." Take the paper to the second spectator. *"Will you write four digits under the first number, please. We'll need three numbers, so I'll write one as well."* You do your writing as described later.

"I will now show my assistant the paper for a single fleeting moment." Flash the paper in front of your helper and hand it back to the spectator, who will add the digits. At the same time your partner writes a number quickly. He or she will have an accurate total in a matter of seconds.

Here is how it works. The first spectator writes any digit (example: 2494). The second spectator does the same (example: 6123). You write the last number. Each of the digits you write in will total 9 when added to the previous number.

Example: Original 2494
          Second   6123
          Yours   <u>3876</u>   (His 6 plus your 3 = 9)

Your assistant need only see the first number. He or she will add the numeral "1" in front of the number and reduce the last digit by 1. The total will be 12493. It will work every time as long as your digits, when added to the previous number, total 9.

Here is how you might adapt this to a mental telepathy test. Allow the first spectator to write his number. Hand it to the spectator seated next to your assistant. In this way, he or she can see the first number. While you start to blindfold the assistant, have the second number written. You write the third number as described. Allow a third spectator to total the digits. This last spectator is now asked to concentrate on the total, *"known only to you and you alone."* Your assistant calls off the digits one at a time.

LEONARDO'S NUMBERS

I am sure that Leonardo Fibonacci never thought that one of his serious works would ever find its way into the art of magic. Fibonacci was a mathematician who lived in the early thirteenth century. A modern-day magician named Royal Heath in 1940 utilized his discovery and introduced it to the magic world.

Mathematicians are familiar with a series of numbers called the Fibonacci Series. Each number in the series is the sum of the two previous numbers. For example, we will start with two single digits, 4 and 9. Add these and we get 13, which when added to 9 gives us 22. This plus the 13 gives us

35, and so on. Here are ten numbers in this series to show you how it works.

$$4$$
$$9$$
$$13$$
$$22$$
$$35$$
$$57$$
$$92 \leftarrow \text{seventh number}$$
$$149$$
$$241$$
$$\underline{390}$$

The total of these ten numbers is 1012. You can arrive at the total of a series of ten Fibonacci numbers by noting the seventh number in the series. Multiply this number by eleven, and you have the total in a moment ($92 \times 11 = 1012$).

Let's use this for an amazing demonstration of rapid calculation. Hand a sheet of paper to one of your spectators and request that he write a single numeral. He is then to pass the paper to the next spectator, who writes another single numeral. Instruct a third spectator to add the first two digits and write the third, and so on until the paper has a series of ten numbers.

You will refrain from writing anything. As the paper goes around the table, you will look for the seventh number. This is all you need. Start to write after calculating quickly. Eleven times the seventh number is your total. You can write this even before the final number has been added. Announce the total in a dramatic manner.

You can also write it as a prediction or, better yet, ask

the last spectator to concentrate on the total and read his mind. This is especially amazing when done for math students.

WATCH YOUR THOUGHTS

What better place is there to find numbers than on your own wrist? Use a watch that has the arabic numbers clearly printed on the face—roman numerals are too confusing. You could borrow a watch or, if none is available, draw a watch face on the side of your menu. This stunt is quite bold, so you must do both effects here immediately following one another. Pick your first spectator.

"There are twelve numerals on the clock face. Please think of any one of them. Now look at the numeral directly opposite the one you chose. Subtract the smaller digit from the larger. You now have a new number. Please write that number on your napkin, fold it, and hand it to me." Place the paper napkin against your forehead as though deep in thought and announce, *"I get the figure five . . . no, I believe it is a six. Am I correct?"* You will be correct, of course: it always works out to six. But go right into the next stage. Hand the watch to another spectator.

"Please look at the watch for a moment. Beginning with number 1, please count around the face and stop at any number you wish. Remember that number. Now go back to number 1 and count around the other way. The 12 will be 2, 11 is 3 and so on. Keep counting so that your count is the same as the first number you stopped at. Now you have a second number. Add this to the original number. Think of the result. Are you concentrating? I believe your total is 14."

This one works all by itself, but do not allow your

spectators too much time to study the clock. Go right to another trick. You might follow this with the Watch Prediction we described earlier.

CALENDAR MAGIC

The father of modern mentalism was a man named Theodore Annemann, whose book *Practical Mental Effects* was published in 1944. Here are a few quick stunts from that book, based on Tom Sellers' excellent analysis of things to do with a calendar.

Have your spectator choose any month on his pocket calendar. He is asked to draw a box around any four dates forming a square (Figure 63). *"Please total the four numbers and tell us the result."* After he has done this, you can tell him the four numbers he selected. Here is how.

			MAY			
SUN	MON	TUE	WED	THU	FRI	SAT
						1
2	3	4	5	6	7	8
9	10	11	12	13	14	15
16	17	18	19	20	21	22
23	24	25	26	27	28	29
30	31					

Figure 63

We will assume he selected the four numbers in our diagram. The total is 60. You will always *divide by four* and *then subtract four*. This will give you the lowest number in the selected series (60 ÷ 4 = 15 - 4 = 11). You can now name the other digits. If you add one you get the next number (12). Add 7 to your result (11 + 7 = 18), and you get the third number. Add one and you have the last number.

Hand the calendar to another spectator. *"Let's try it again. This time pick another month. Don't tell me which month you chose. Please draw a box around three numbers in a vertical line."* (Figure 64.) He is to give you the total. This time you *divide by 3* to give you the *middle* number (example: Total is 63. 63 ÷ 3 = 21).

To find the other numbers, subtract 7 (21 - 7 = 14) for the top number and add 7 for the bottom number (21 + 7 = 28).

			JUNE			
SUN	MON	TUE	WED	THU	FRI	SAT
		1	2	3	4	5
6	7	8	9	10	11	12
13	14	15	16	17	18	19
20	21	22	23	24	25	26
27	28	29	30			

Figure 64

NUMBER GAMES

Here are just a few entertaining things to do with paper and pencil.

I Win   Play a game with your neighbor. Using one sheet of paper, take turns writing a number between 1 and 10 in a column. Add each number as you go, and announce the running total each time. The goal is to be the first to reach 100. You will always win.

Remember this simple set of key numbers. 12-23-34-45-56-67-78-89. You will note that each digit is one higher than the previous one so that they are easy to remember. Keep the total running until you hit any one of these key numbers. From that point on your digits depend upon what he has written. Always add a number that when added to his last figure equals *eleven*. As soon as you hit 89 you win automatically. You will win in any case.

Challenges   *"Can you arrange eight 4s in such a way that they add up to 176?"*   Let your spectator try a few times before you reveal the method. Arrange them this way.

$$
\begin{array}{r}
44 \\
44 \\
44 \\
+\ 44 \\
\hline
176
\end{array}
$$

"Now arrange all the digits 0123456789 so that they will add up to 180." To do this write them in a vertical line beginning with number 1 down to 5, and come up with the 6 through 0.

$$
\begin{array}{r}
10 \\
29 \\
38 \\
47 \\
+\ 56 \\
\hline
180
\end{array}
$$

Final Arrangement   Arrange 8 and 8 so that they equal 10000.

8
8   (Turn sideways)

3

Pocket Prestidigitation

Money Magic

PENETRATING COIN

Use a quarter or a half dollar for this pretty effect. A coin placed under a napkin will come right through the cloth. This will take a bit of practice, but it is worth the effort.

Bring the coin under the center of a cloth napkin as shown in Figure 65. Make sure that one end of the cloth is hanging down (A) and one corner rests on your arm. (B)

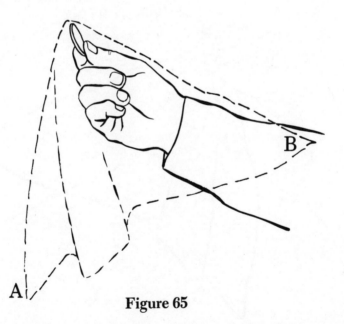

Figure 65

Your left hand adjusts the coin through the outside of the cloth so that the shape of the coin can be seen. During this adjustment your right thumb pinches a small tuck of cloth and presses it against the coin as shown in Figure 66.

Your left hand moves to the front of the cloth and picks up point A, pulling it back to your right arm so that it overlaps B. The coin is now seen and shown. *"It is still here"* (Figure 67).

Your left hand now takes both corners A and B and brings them back down away from you so that they both hang in front of your hand. The coin is now outside the napkin and is being held under the cloth by your right thumb and forefinger. Remove your left hand and shake the cloth so that all four ends hang down (Figure 68).

Your left hand now comes back to the bottom corners and begins to twist the napkin. As the napkin gets closer the

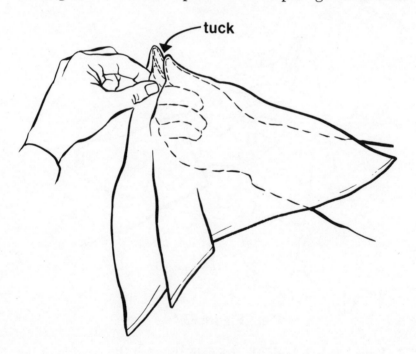

tuck

Figure 66

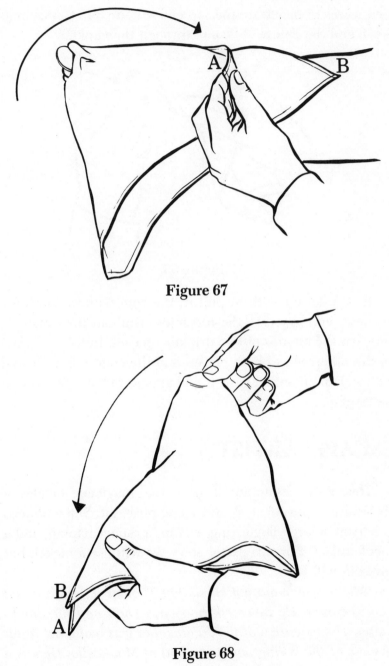

Figure 67

Figure 68

coin seems to penetrate the top end (Figure 69). Gently pull down and the coin will "come through the napkin."

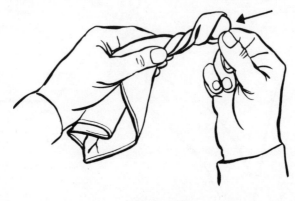

Figure 69

If you do not wish to pull it, the coin will remain for a moment, entrapped in the top folds. You can then place it between the mouths of two drinking glasses. Invert one glass on the other. Shake both glasses and the coin will drop free with a clank. In either case, it will appear to have penetrated the napkin.

ESCAPE ARTIST

This is an example of how the magician tackles a physically impossible task and accomplishes it. You will need to borrow a large finger ring, a coin, a dinner napkin, and a handkerchief. For this patter story we will use a nickel, but any coin will work.

"Many people did not know that Thomas Jefferson was a great inventor. He invented the swivel chair and the dumbwaiter. The invention of the dumbwaiter was really the result of some of the boring parties he had at Monticello. Here is a

picture of the house." Turn the nickel to show the house. Point to any spot. *"There is the room where he had his parties. Can you see the dumbwaiter? If you can, ask him for some coffee."* Spread the handkerchief flat on the table as you patter. *"The dumbwaiter was a sort of elevator in the kitchen that took dishes up and down. To escape from a room, one could hide in the dumbwaiter and wind up down below. Jefferson often used it to escape from those dull parties. Here is how he did it."*

Place the nickel in the center of the handkerchief. Gather the four ends and pass them through the opening of the large ring. Pull the ring down so that the coin is trapped in a little sack at the bottom.

"Jefferson is trapped inside." Spread the handkerchief on the table again. Turn it over so that the coin is on top of the ring. Its shape will be seen through the cloth (Figure 70).

"If you will all hold on to the corners, I will show you

X

Figure 70

how Tom slipped away from the parties. He hid in the dumbwaiter." Cover the handkerchief with the dinner napkin so that no one can see what you will be doing under the cloth. Reach underneath and pass the edge of the cloth marked X through the ring from underneath. Ask for some slack if you need it. You will find that if you pull it up close to the ring, you have formed a small opening. Work the coin through this opening. It should come out easily. Once you have it, pull the coin with one hand, the napkin with the other hand, and bring both hands up with a flourish. *"While everyone was upstairs at the party, Tom got away downstairs with the maid."* Show the coin and return the ring, handkerchief, and napkin.

COINS THROUGH THE TABLE

Before we leave the topic of penetrations we must consider another classic trick. This spectacular coin magic is called Coins Through the Table, and many professionals perform it. They do one or another of the many variations, most of which require sleight-of-hand ability. We promised no intricate sleights, so we now offer a very simple but effective version: we will pass a handful of coins through a solid tabletop.

Your left hand is in your lap secretly holding a bunch of coins in your palm. The more coins used, the better the trick will look.

"Every table made in the United States is made with a secret soft spot—I'll bet you didn't know that." Close your left hand and, with coins held tightly so they do not rattle, bring your left fist up and knock on various spots on the tabletop. Pretend to find a spot about ten inches in front of you. *"Did you hear that?"*

Bring your left hand back to your lap and open the palm. Position the back of your right wrist so that it sits in your left hand, covering the coins. If your left hand is cupped slightly it makes for better sound (Figure 71). The fingers of your left hand encircle your right wrist. Bring your right hand up, closed in a fist, being held by the left. *"That was the right soft spot and I'll prove it with these."* Shake both hands up and down a few times. The coins in your left palm will make noise and it will appear to be coming from your right hand.

Figure 71

"A bunch of money, right through the soft spot." As you say this, bring your left hand under the table, and at the same time strike your right palm flat on the spot you selected. Your left hand hits the table from underneath in the same relative position. The sound of the striking coins will add to the effect.

Bring your left hand from under the table and allow the

coins to dribble onto the table. *"Be careful not to put any dishes on that spot, or they'll fall right through."*

KNOTTY AFFAIR

Here is a principle that can be used for many different tricks. This is a method of producing a coin or finding one that has just vanished. You will need a napkin and a duplicate of the coin that you will borrow. Let's assume it is a quarter.

As you pick up a napkin, secretly hide the quarter behind the corner at your right hand (Figure 72). The other hand picks up the diagonally opposite end of the napkin and you rotate both hands away from your body. This will loosely twist the napkin, rope fashion, into a tube next to the coin. Lift that end of the tube and gently relax pressure on the coin. The quarter will slide into the center of the napkin (Figure 73). Tie both ends into a loose knot and gently set the napkin on the table or into a flat plate. The coin is secure inside. (Be sure to practice this a few times before you perform it for friends.)

When performing, casually pick up the napkin, add the coin and start to rotate the ends as you talk. *"When I was young I remember seeing a magician who did a most amazing thing. He tied a knot into a napkin just as I am doing."* Set the napkin on a plate a bit to your right or left but not directly in front of you. *"Then he borrowed a large coin. May I borrow a quarter from someone?"* Set the quarter on the table about six inches in front of you, in readiness for the Lap Vanish we described earlier.

"He held the coin above the napkin like this." Pretend to remove the coin from the table, but actually drop it into

Figure 72

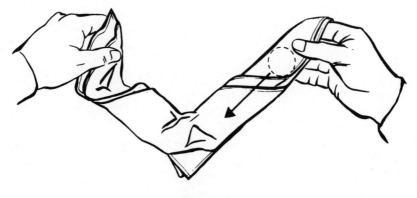

Figure 73

your lap as the hand slides back to the edge of the table (Figure 74). Keep your fingers in the same position as if you actually were holding the coin. Raise your hand above the knot (Figure 75) and rub the fingers together gently. *"And with a bit of magic, the coin passed invisibly through the air and into the knot."* Show your hand empty.

Lift up the napkin by one corner and strike it against the plate so that the coin is heard inside. Hand the napkin to a spectator to open. *"I saw this done only once, and from that day to this I could never figure out how he did it."*

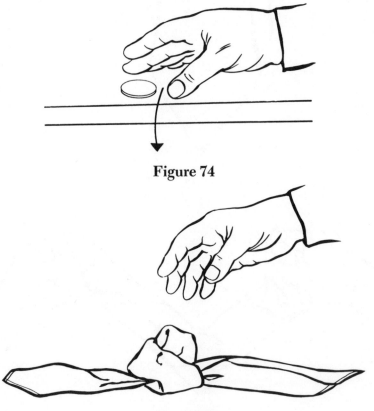

Figure 74

Figure 75

QUICK COIN VANISH

This technique will enable you to vanish one or many coins, depending upon what you want to do. Practice it—it is great for impromptu magic. Use a handkerchief or dinner napkin. If you use a single coin it will be easier to get rid of later. If you choose to vanish a bunch of coins, you will have to bring them back again quickly. Here is how this works.

Your dinner napkin is spread open on the table diagonally in front of you. Place the coin or coins in the center. Fold the bottom end up away from you forming a triangle as in Figure 76.

The right-hand corner A is brought to your left and dropped half way between the two left ends (position X). Figure 77 shows this step. Pick up corner B and bring it across to your right at point Y.

If you lift the napkin, pulling A to the left and B to your

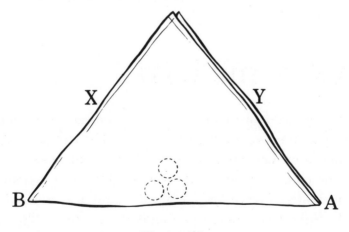

Figure 76

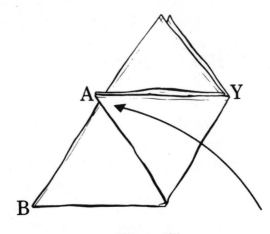

Figure 77

right, the coin or coins vanish. They are trapped in a curious pocket made by the folding process.

If you are using one coin, rotate the ends of the napkin as you did in the previous trick. This forms a tube, and your coin can slide down into your hand quietly. If using a bunch of coins, gently tie a knot in the napkin without jingling the coins. You now reverse the trick by saying a few magic words: *"The check is in the mail."* Open the napkin and the coins are back where they began.

COIN IN THE WATER

Any ventriloquist will tell you that the ear is easy to fool. You need the eye to help the ear tell where a sound is coming from. Let's fool the ear with this coin vanish.

The coin is held under the center of a napkin or handkerchief (Figure 78). A glass of water is in your left hand. Bring the coin and handkerchief over the glass, covering it. Your left thumb tips the glass slightly toward your fingertips as you drop the coin, so that it hits the side of the glass near your thumb (X). It will then bounce quietly into your left hand. Your right hand removes the glass still wrapped in the handkerchief and sets it on the table. The left hand casually moves away. Pull the handkerchief off the glass and *Voila!* The coin is gone!

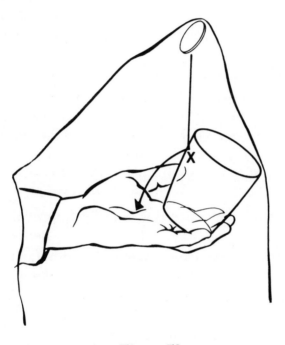

Figure 78

ELBOW ON THE TABLE

It isn't good manners to put your elbow on the table, but when you do this trick you will have to get into that position. This is a favorite of California magician Joe Berg, who presents it just this way:

COIN GAGS AND STUNTS

Borrow a coin. Drop it on the table in front of you. Cover the coin with the middle fingers of your right hand. In the meantime you bring your left elbow onto the table and rest your head against the left palm. *"Press down on the coin through my fingers."*

As soon as he reaches out to follow your instructions, pick up the coin with your right hand and bring it to your left sleeve. Do this with a quick motion as you say, *"No, not that hand, the other hand."* This action and the words act as your misdirection while you drop the coin into the left sleeve. Bring the right hand back to the table as if the coin were still there.

As he presses your fingertips, casually drop your left hand to your side. The coin slides into your hand. Retrieve it and bring it up under the table, snapping it with a click on the bottom. *"You pressed too hard; it went right through."* Bring the coin from under the table. *"You see, coins dissolve easily. I'll show you what I mean."*

Put the elbow back on the table and rest your chin on your left hand. Pick up the coin with your right hand and rub it into your left arm between the elbow and wrist. Let go of the coin, and it drops to the table. Pick it up with the *left* hand. Put it into the right hand, again rest your chin on your left hand, repeat the rubbing action, and drop it again. This time the left hand picks up the coin and pretends to put it into the right hand. As you again go through the motion of resting your chin on your left hand, drop the coin into your coat collar. The right hand rubs the left arm again, then "discovers" that the coin has dissolved. You can retrieve it when no one is looking.

Nickel Through   Borrow a business card or use a small piece of paper. Place a dime in the center of the card and draw around it with a pencil so there is a circle the same size as the dime. Tear out the center so you now have a hole in the card. Fold the card in half widthwise and drop a nickel in the center of the fold.

You can now bet that on your command the nickel will fall through the hole. Impossible as it appears, the nickel will go through if you hold the card by the ends and bring both hands together upward and inward. The hole becomes elongated, and the coin drops through.

A Head for Money   Secretly wet the side of a penny and push it against your forehead. It will stay there for a moment. Take it off quickly, before it falls, and then press it against the forehead of the person opposite you. Do not leave the coin, but take it away. Pretend it is still on his head. *"Can you remove the coin without touching it?"* Watch his face and have fun with others as he wrinkles his forehead and shakes his head about trying to get it off.

Coin Balance   Hide a paper match in your lap, resting it on your knee. Pick up a large coin such as a half dollar or quarter and try to balance it on your flat palm. Set the coin on edge facing your audience and place it at the second joint of the ring finger. It will fall. Rub the coin on your lap and bring it up to the table again for a second try. Another failure.

On the third try, you have secretly picked up the match between the middle and ring fingers. Rest the coin against the match (Figure 79). From the front it looks as if it were balanced.

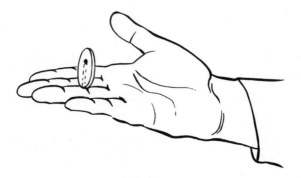

Figure 79

Inflation   Hold up a quarter and show it around. *"It's such a shame that this isn't worth twenty-five cents anymore. It buys only fifteen cents' worth. It's enough to make poor Tom Jefferson cry."* Water drips from behind the coin as you squeeze it.

The secret is simple. Surreptitiously wet a small piece of paper napkin, ball it, and hold it behind the coin. Squeeze and watch the coin cry.

Balancing Stunt   You can balance a dime on the edge of a dollar bill. Use a new bill if you can. Fold it in half lengthwise, making a sharp crease. Now fold it in half the other way as in Figure 80.

Place the dime on the corner you have just created (A). Gently lift the bill with the thumb and forefingers of each hand, one on each side. As you bring your hands apart the coin will balance on the crease (B).

MONEY FROM MONEY

When the subject is money, most people will pay close attention to what you do and say. Here is a nice way to introduce some coin or bill magic.

You must have a coin in your hand to begin with—use a quarter if you have one. Don't go out of your way in trying to hide it. The coin is merely held in your right hand, resting between the first and second joints of your middle and ring fingers. No one will see it unless you get self-conscious.

"I am going to show you how to make some money. May I borrow a dollar bill? In our society we never use our own money when we can get a loan."

Take the borrowed bill with your left hand and place it casually in your right hand over the quarter. If you turn your wrist over you can show the underside of the bill without exposing the coin. Turn the hand palm up again.

"It takes money to make money. Look at how George is watching me." Your right index finger comes up and over the

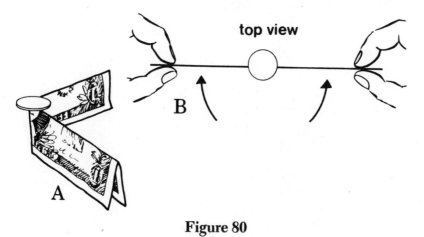

Figure 80

bill so that it rests alongside your right thumb. The thumb and finger are on each side of the face on the bill (Figure 81). Your left hand takes the corner of the bill (X) and rolls it toward your body, running over the index finger (Figure 82). The bill is now green side up. Slide the bill forward a bit so that you can fold it in half by bringing it away from you under the index finger again.

"To double your money you can fold it. But I won't tamper with it, since it is your money. I just want to make a bit of profit. Like twenty-five percent."

Figure 81

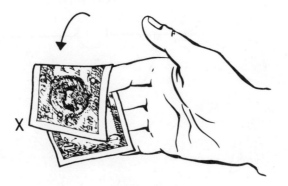

Figure 82

Move your right thumb to the edge of the bill near you. Shake the bill slightly over your opened left palm and allow the quarter to drop out. Hand the bill back to its owner. *"I knew that if I started doing things with money I would get a little interest."*

CLEAN GETAWAY

It was easy to produce a quarter, and we can vanish it again just as easily using the same dollar bill. This is known to magicians as a Coin Fold. It can be done with a piece of paper but is more dramatic when done with money. Using the quarter and dollar bill from the earlier trick, follow the diagrams and learn this one.

1. Place the coin in the center of the bill covering the Washington portrait. Fold the bottom half up just to the edge of the numeral 1 on the face of the bill (Figure 83).

2. The sides of the bill are folded behind the bill, which

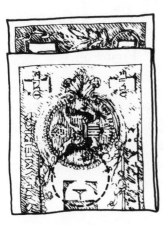

Figure 83

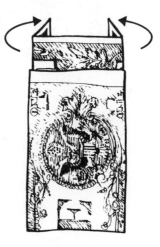

Figure 84

will give you an open packet at the top. Fold by making a crease just *under* the words at the left and *over* the words at the right. You will have to hold the coin securely through the package as you do this (Figure 84).

3. There is about half an inch of the black side showing above the green folds. Fold this back and away from you so that you have an envelope holding the coin (Figure 85).

4. The spectator sees the front of this package, which should look like Figure 86. While the coin is apparently locked in this envelope, there is actually a secret opening at the top.

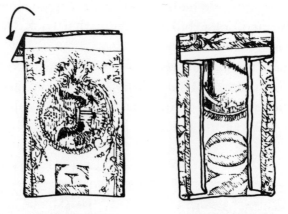

Figure 85   **Figure 86**

5. Strike the package against a drinking glass so that the coin can be heard. Turn the parcel upside down, and the weight of the coin will cause it to slide quietly into your right hand. Take the bill with the other hand and set it down gently on a saucer nearby. The coin is gone.

TRANSPOSITION

By using several principles we can create new magic. In this case we will cause a quarter to fly from one package to another. A transposition is created by combining a vanish with a production.

Borrow two one-dollar bills. Be prepared beforehand with a quarter in your hand, which you will introduce secretly. The first bill is taken in the right hand, and you show both sides by using the Money from Money move. Start to fold the bill as you did in that trick, but not exactly in half. You will fold it just as you folded the bill in the Clean Getaway trick. The difference is that you secretly put a coin into the envelope instead of taking one out. Set the package on the table at your left.

"This is a little envelope which we will use in a moment. Now may I borrow a coin? A quarter is the right size and, besides, I need an eagle." This coin is placed in the center of the bill openly and you do your coin fold again. You set this package at your right, but do not steal the coin.

"You probably wondered why I needed an eagle. This eagle is a flyer." Point to the bill at your right. *"I will now cause the quarter to fly from here to the other side."* Point to the bill at your left. *"Watch!"* Snap your fingers. *"It is done. There is now an eagle at my left. The hard part is getting him to fly back. Watch."* Snap again. Lift the package at the right and hit it against a glass so the coin is heard. Tip it and steal the coin before you put it down again.

At this point nothing has happened and the audience is amused at your nonsense. *"I suppose you don't believe me. I'll have to do it again. Watch."* Snap your fingers *"Go."*

Push the left-hand package to one spectator. *"Will you open the envelope and see if he's there?"* Push the other bill to another spectator. *"You can keep this; it's empty."*

TWO BILLS TO ONE

I recently had dinner with Ed Mishell, past national president of the Society of American Magicians, and as always we talked about magic. We were discussing an old bill-folding trick, when Ed reached for his wallet and took out two folded dollar bills. *"I have a better one,"* he said. In an instant he caused the two bills to change into a single bill—one vanished. He graciously explained it to me, saying it was a variation of the old trick modernized by our mutual friend Pat Mollo. Here's how it goes.

Only one bill is used, and you should have it folded and ready before you do your trick. It should be a crisp new bill so you can fold it neatly. Do this ahead of time, although with practice you can do it under the table, using a menu for support.

1. Washington is looking up at you. Crease the bill sharply as you fold it in half the long way. Open it again and crease it once more, folding it in half widthwise.

2. With the bill still folded in half, neatly tear a slit about an inch long through the center of George's picture. You can get the right length by tearing from the center fold to the edge of the picture frame (Figure 87).

3. With Washington still watching you, refold the bill along the long crease. Then crease the bill sharply from the right side of the slit, at an angle toward the *top* of the bill, so that it passes through the letter *I* in "America." This leaves

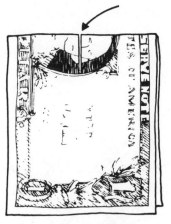

Figure 87

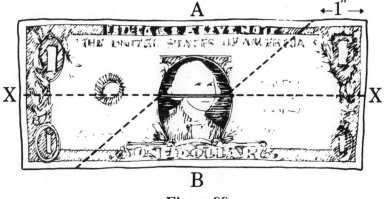

Figure 88

an inch on the top right side of the crease. Do the same on the bottom, folding from the left end of the slit *down* toward the bottom left side of the bill an inch from the end (Figure 88).

4. The bill is now creased properly. Open it again. Fold it in half horizontally. Your thumb and index finger holds each end of the dollar at point X in Figure 88 (A is folded under B). Gently push the two ends together. The slit will open,

exposing a hole in the bill. When the two sides of the slit come together and touch one another, turn your hands so that your thumbs turn up toward the ceiling. The bill will fold, forming a crisscross pattern (Figure 89).

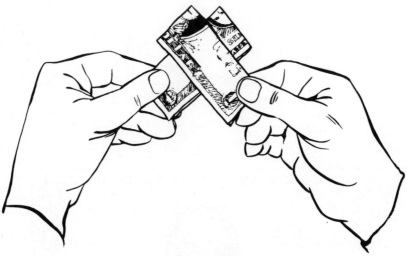

Figure 89

You now have what looks like two bills folded across one another. Hold this with the left thumb at the bottom of the crossed ends as you bring the bill to the table.

"It's really a shame how the economy has changed in recent times. Years ago I could take two dollars and buy food that was worth two dollars. Now I pay two dollars . . . and get only a dollar's worth." Pull your thumbs away from one another to open the bill to the horizontal fold. Open it flat by snapping each end. The slit vanishes into the portrait. Put the dollar into your pocket.

INSTANT CASH

If you ask magician Arnold Freed to do a trick, you can bet that he'll roll up his sleeves, rub his hands together, and come up with a shower of dollar bills from nowhere. You can do it too.

You will need to prepare five or six bills in advance. Put them all together, one atop the other, and fold them in half. Now fold them in half again twice more, making a small roll. The roll is placed in the crook of your left arm. Pull back some of the cloth from your coat or shirt to cover the roll and bend the left arm slightly (Figure 90). You are ready to perform.

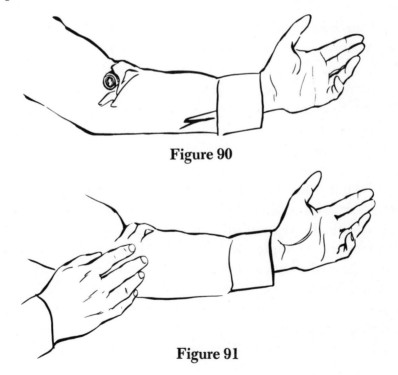

Figure 90

Figure 91

Show your right hand empty while at the same time pulling your right sleeve back with your left hand. Pull back the cloth from the crook of your right arm. Now show your left hand empty by opening the left palm, while your right hand pulls the left sleeve back. As you straighten your arm, the right hand will steal the roll of bills. All attention is on the left palm (Figure 91).

Bring both hands together and rub them vigorously, allowing the money to dribble down to the table one bill at a time. It is a very effective trick, and, as I said earlier, money tricks always attract attention.

TORN AND RESTORED BILL

Your friend will be laughing on the outside but quite apprehensive on the inside when you borrow money and start tearing it in half. Here is how you can do it safely.

Secretly crumple a dollar bill into a small ball. This is held in your left hand with your three bottom fingers lightly curled around it

"Lend me a dollar and I'll show you something interesting. Wait a minute—this one looks like a counterfeit."

Take the bill and hold it between your hands. Press your left thumbnail against the middle of the bill. Pull the bill away with the right hand and you'll get a tearing sound. Immediately crumple the bill in the right hand and reveal the piece in the left hand. It will appear that you tore his bill in half. *"These two pieces are not even worth fifty cents apiece."* Show two small pieces, one in each hand. *"You look worried. Okay, I'll fix it."*

Extend your left hand to the person on your left. The

right hand moves to the edge of the table. *"Please blow gently on the bill."* Now bring your left hand back to the edge of the table and offer the bill in your right hand to a person on your right.*"Please blow on the other piece."* As you do this, secretly drop the ball from the left hand into your lap.

With both hands closed bring them to the center of the table in front of you. Push your palms together and rub the money between your hands. *"I don't want to rub you the wrong way. So here is your dollar in one piece again."* Open it slowly and hand it back to the spectator.

PRODUCING THE TIP

The reason that I don't like dessert is that it comes so close to the check. By the time it has arrived you have probably astounded your friends by levitating a dinner roll, or perhaps the saltshaker has passed through the table and you've done some mind reading. Now comes the dinner check and if someone else grabs it, paying the tip is up to you. Your last trick can be a reputation maker if you produce some money.

"I'll take care of the tip with a little magic." The spectators do not know that you have prepared for this by slipping a small roll of two or three one-dollar bills under your watchband. Pick up a paper napkin with your left hand and give it a shake to open it. If you hold it between your thumb and index fingers it will open in front of your palm, hiding the money under the watchband.

The right-hand thumb and middle finger snap a hole in the center of the napkin. Index and middle fingers go into the hole and pull the money out of its hiding place through the opening. *"This should cover the tip."* Spread the bills and drop them loosely on the table. That's what I would call ending your act with style.

DOLLAR-BILL GAGS AND STUNTS

Breaking Bread Have your spectator hold a breadstick by each end. Fold a dollar bill lengthwise, holding it loosely at one end between your thumb and middle finger. Strike the breadstick in the center. Nothing will happen. On the second try, secretly extend your index finger as you strike again. The finger breaks the stick without being seen.

Delicate Balance Accordion-pleat a dollar bill, making sharp creases on each fold. Set it as a bridge between two glasses. Now you can balance a third glass on the bill (Figure 92).

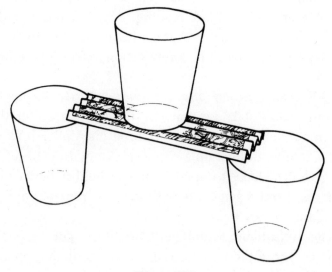

Figure 92

Pure Corn *"If you hand me a single dollar bill I will show you how to double your money."* Fold the bill in half and show it. *"Now you can see it in creases."* Show a creased bill—and then duck so you won't get hit when the spectator throws a plate at you for that corny gag.

A Safe Bet Have the spectator remove a bill from his pocket without looking at it, and bet that he cannot name three of the digits in its serial number. He will guess two but not three in most cases. The odds are in your favor that he cannot do it.

One to Five Bet that you can make a one-dollar bill into a five. Roll the bill the long way so that it resembles a piece of rope. You can then shape it on the table into the numeral 5.

Miracles with Matches

MATCHBOOK DIVINATION *

Although we will treat this effect as a test of your unique sense of touch, it can be adapted easily to a telepathic trick. Or you can pretend that sound waves play a part in the trick. Have fun with it, no matter which way you present it.

You will need to borrow three packages of book matches. Make sure they all have different advertising designs. As you receive each one, lift it and pretend to be weighing it in your hand. Before you drop it onto the table again secretly push the flap firmly toward the bottom so that it locks tightly in place. After all three packets have been "weighed," turn your back.

"I will turn my back for a moment so that I can't see what you are doing. Please pick up one pack and remove a single match. Put the match in your pocket, close the flap, and leave the pack on the table."

When this has been done, turn back to the table. Pick up the packets one by one, hefting each one again. As you lift each pack, have your thumb on the opening side, which should be facing away from you. Gently pull back on the thumb. Only one flap will come back easily; the others will remain tightly locked. The loose flap is on the package from which he took the match.

Hold it up to your ear as if you heard something. *"I think this one sounds as if it has a match missing."*

* Tricks using matches and cigarettes are not recommended for children.

GHOST MATCH

One of the things I enjoy most is lecturing to my fellow magicians around the country. I show them card tricks, sleight-of-hand techniques, and some table magic. This particular trick seems to be the best received in my lecture. If you follow it with the Decap trick I will describe later, you will have a nice, logical routine.

Borrow a pack of matches. Hold it in your left hand with the closing flap under your thumb. *"Do you know how many matches are in this pack? You don't? I'll hold the pack while you count them. Make an accurate count, please."*

Your right hand opens the flap and bends it away from you. At the same time, your left thumb slides up toward the head of one of the matches. The thumb secretly pulls the match straight back, allowing it to ride along the finger so that the head is now positioned at the first joint (Figure 93). The thumb goes back to the base of the matches as the left

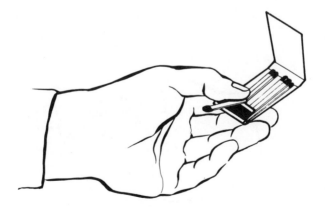

Figure 93

index and middle fingers clip the cover between them. All this is done casually in one motion.

Extend the left hand for the spectator to count his matches. *"How many have you counted?"* Let's assume he counted eight matches. *"Eight? Fine. If I take one away, that will leave how many? Right. Seven matches."* As you speak, pull out one match and set it in front of you on the table about three inches from the edge. Close the cover of the pack by releasing your left index finger so that it snaps loose. Your right hand takes the cover and draws it back toward your body and into your left palm (Figure 94). This puts the extra match back where it belongs. The pack is now flat on the left palm. The right index finger tucks the flap *under* the matches and locks it. Place the matches on the table. *"Put your finger on top of the seven matches so that I can't take one out or put one in."* There are really eight matches in the pack because the spectator counted one less than were actually there in the first place.

Pretend to pick up the single match by sliding it back to the edge of the table. It goes into your lap as you bring your

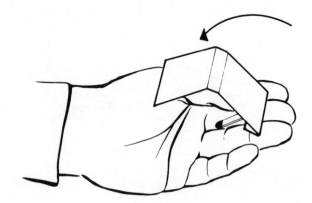

Figure 94

hand up above the spectator's. Rub your fingers together. *"Did you feel anything just then?"* He doesn't feel a thing. *"The match just returned. Count them, please."* Do not underestimate the effect of this trick.

Should you have a chance to tamper with the matches before you do the trick, you could burn one match by pulling it back, lighting it with another match, and blowing it out. (Be very careful not to set off the whole pack.) With the matches prepared this way you pick up the pack and pull back the burned match. After the spectator counts the matches, you tear out one and hand over the pack for safekeeping. Burn the single match, blow it out immediately, and after it cools vanish it.

When the pack is opened the spectator finds the single burned match. *"Feel it—it's still hot, isn't it?"* If you ask the question that way you'll be surprised at how many people answer, *"Yes, it is!"*

DECAP

Whenever I perform close-up magic I do this effect after the Ghost Match, since it is a natural follow-up: I have a match in my lap, and the spectator is holding the pack.

Under the table, secretly tear the head off the match. You won't need the rest of it. Pinch this piece between the index and middle fingers of your right hand. No one can see it, so don't worry about hiding it.

"May I have a single match, please? Tear out any one of them." After this is done, take the match with your left hand. Your left thumb and forefinger cover the head part. *"We won't need the rest of the matches. Open your hand, please."*

Bring both of your hands together. The bottom of the

whole match should touch the space between the index and middle fingers of the right hand. Put your right thumb on the torn end and with a sudden motion snap your hands apart. Drop the tiny match head into the spectator's palm. *"We'll need two pieces. You take the head and I'll take the rest."* It will appear as though you just tore the match.

"Wait a minute. I gave you the wrong part. I'll take the head and you take the rest." Your right hand takes away the little piece. Your left hand places the whole match into the spectator's palm. The head is still covered secretly by your left thumb. Using your right hand, close the spectator's fingers over the match. *"Close your hand."* As soon as the fingers start to close, take your left hand away.

Show the little piece again, setting it in front of you on the table. Pretend to pick it up again, but secretly drop it into your lap. *"I think I'm still wrong. You can have the head. In fact, you can have the whole match."* Make a throwing motion and open your hand to show that the head is gone. *"Open your hand!"* Much to the spectator's amazement, the match seems completely restored.

Don't let anyone talk you into repeating either of the two tricks: they lose the surprise factor, which is half the fun.

FULL PACK

A brand-new pack of matches has twenty matches in it. Most people know this but never stop to think about it. Combining this knowledge with our old friend, the nine principle, we can do a cute divination stunt.

"That looks like a new pack of matches. I hope you're playing with a full pack. Take them under the table and tear out a small bunch—no more than ten matches." If one or two

matches were missing from the full pack, restrict the number of matches torn out to five at most.

"I have no way of knowing how many matches are left in the pack. Please count them. Keep the extra matches out of sight in your lap. Did you get a two-digit number? Good. Add those two digits and you have a new number. Tear out that many more matches." (If there were 12 left, he adds the digits 1 and 2 and tears out three matches.) *"I still have no way of knowing how many matches are left. Take out some more matches and hold them in your right hand. Close the packet and hold that in your left hand. Bring both hands to the table."*

Wait until this has been done. *"I shall now attempt to tell you either how many matches you hold in your hand or how many are left in the pack. Which do you prefer?"* Let us assume he requests the number in his hand. *"May I have the pack, please. I need one match."* Tear out a single match and strike it on the pack. While you are doing that you secretly count all the matches, including the one you tore out. Subtract that number from nine and you have the total in the hand. Pass the struck match over your hand and announce the number.

If the spectator asks that you divine the number remaining in the pack, you need a quick glance in his hand. *"Open your hand—I need one match."* Count them quickly and subtract from nine as you take a single match. Hold it against your forehead as though you were deep in thought. Announce the number dramatically.

INVISIBLE DICE

Using your own package of matches, casually left lying on the table, you can enjoy a bit of nonsense with this match trick. You will also need an invisible pair of dice, but of course any spectator can lend that to you.

Prepare ahead of time for the trick by using a sharp pencil to write the numbers 1 through 6 on the heads of six front-row matches. Close the pack and leave it lying on the table nearby. In case someone needs a match, light an unmarked one for him so as not to disturb your setup.

"Does anyone have a pair of dice? I need a large, invisible set of dice. How about that pair in front of you?" Point to any spectator. *"Please pick up the dice and shake them up a bit. Careful, you just dropped one. Shake them out onto the table so we can all see them. What is the total on the dice?"*

We'll assume he or she names *"seven,"* which is most common. *"I'm a bit too far away to see them. What is the number on that one?"* Point anywhere. *"Five?"* (Or whatever is named.)

Pick up your matches and tear out two: the ones marked five and two to total seven. Strike them both at the same time, rubbing the side away from the numbers as you light them. *"Maybe this will help me see better. I don't see the dice, but this is very interesting. The matches are getting red-hot."* Hold them straight so they will burn hotter. As soon as each head gets red-hot—it takes about fifteen seconds—blow it out. The heads will turn white. Revolve them slowly, exposing the black writing on the white head. *"You're right. Five and two are seven."*

In the unlikely case of the number twelve being named, simply light the number six match. Hold it up and say, *"Six and six are twelve. That's odd. This one says six also."*

You can use this principle to write any small prediction numbers, letters of the alphabet, or small designs. As you will see, the writing must be done with a sharp pencil.

MATCH GAGS, STUNTS, BETCHAS

Which Is Heavier? To everyone's surprise, sleight-of-hand artist Derek Dingle used this old gag on the Barbara Walters TV show recently. Hand your spectator a cigarette lighter and a pack of matches, one in each hand. *"Which one is heavier?"* He will pick the cigarette lighter. *"Wrong."* Take the lighter from him. *"The matches must be heavier, because this is the lighter."* Do a good trick to make up for this gag, which is so awful it is funny.

Two for One Split a paper match from the bottom to just below the head. Tuck it behind the other matches until someone asks for a light. Strike the match and as you offer it, separate it. Each part of the divided head retains its own flame, and you appear to have produced an extra match.

Dollar Light You can light a paper match on a dollar bill. Place a new dollar bill flat on the table. Press firmly on the head as you draw the match quickly across the whole length of the bill. (Don't bet on this one until you've tried it to get the knack.)

Blowout Hold a lighted match behind a drinking glass. Blow directly on the front of the glass at the center. The air stream will run around the glass and extinguish the match.

Match Betcha   *"I'll bet I can light a match underwater."* If someone takes the bet, hand him a glass of water. Light a match under it.

Off with His Head   You can tell this story with paper matches, but a wooden match is better if you have one. Light the match and wait until it gets red-hot before blowing it out.

   "This is Pierre. He is the famous Frenchman who was on a diet and refused Marie Antoinette's famous order to eat cake. They decided to hang him. So they got some rope"—pretend to take a hair from your head and tie it around the head of the match—*"and were about to execute him when Marie gave him a last chance to change his mind. 'No!' he said bravely. So Marie gave the order. 'Off with his head!' "* At that point you are holding the match between the thumb and middle fingers at the bottom. Pull back the invisible thread as the right fingernail flicks the match at a spot just next to the thumb. The match head will fly off comically.

Through the Sleeve   Hold a lighted match—preferably a wooden one—as described in the previous stunt. Raise the match high above your head. Blow into your left sleeve and flick your right fingernail at the same time. It gives the appearance that you have blown in your sleeve to extinguish the match.

Cigarette Things

PERKY CIGARETTE

This mini-illusion is almost perfect when seen from the front—it will look like pure sleight of hand. Make sure that there is no one sitting on either side of you when you perform it.

Borrow a cigarette, taking it from the spectator with your right hand. Position the bottom of the cigarette at the tips of your thumb, ring, and little finger (Figure 95). The other two fingers rest alongside of the thumb, so that it appears to be held by all the fingers.

Figure 95

The left hand picks up a dinner napkin by one corner. *"Now you see it."* Place the napkin in front of the cigarette and bring it back toward your body as if you were covering the cigarette. The two free fingers of your right hand stand upright under the center of the cloth. The other fingers tip the cigarette back toward your body horizontally. You apparently have a cigarette under the cloth, held in a vertical position (Figure 96).

Figure 96

"Now you don't. Watch it pop." As you say this, snap the cigarette forward to the middle of the cloth so that your left fingers all touch one another through the napkin. From the front it will look as though the cigarette popped through the cloth. Pull it up with your left hand and drop it onto the table. Shake the cloth and spread it out. *"No hole in the middle."*

A LITTLE STATIC

I have been doing this trick for many years, but I enjoyed it most one evening when I saw game manufacturer and magic buff Bob Reiss perform it. Over dinner in Chicago Bob was explaining how static electricity can help magicians. A young lady sitting next to him was fascinated with the trick and asked if she could try it. She ran her finger the wrong way, but Bob was still able to accomplish the trick you will see here. The lady thought she did it herself and was eagerly looking forward to trying it on her friends the next day at lunch.

Bob and I, of course, knew it would not work, and we laughed all night picturing that poor woman trying to explain to her friends, *"I know it works, I did it last night."* Here is the trick.

Borrow a cigarette and set it on the table in front of you, making sure there are no obstructions, such as crumbs, on the surface. Place your index finger on the table and explain, *"It is really wonderful how science works to create magic. Static electricity is a perfect example. Watch the cigarette."* Rub your index finger on your left sleeve a few times as if trying to get an electrical charge. Place the finger in front of the cigarette and move it back and forth a few times (Figure 97). The cigarette stays where it is—nothing happens.

Rub your finger on the sleeve again and repeat the movement on the table. On the third try, all eyes will be on the cigarette. As you move your finger forward, blow gently on the cigarette. It will mysteriously roll to follow your finger. *"There it goes; it's charged up now."*

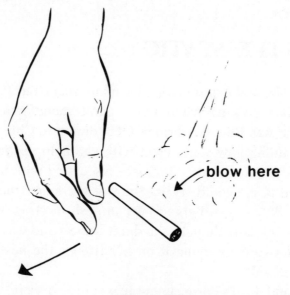

Figure 97

On that evening with Bob Reiss, the lady made the basic error of pulling her finger toward herself. So Bob gently blew the cigarette right into her lap.

You can also use a soda straw for this one, if no cigarette is available.

CIGARETTE GO!

This one must be done with the person seated to your right if you are right-handed. Turn your chair so that you are facing him. *"Please cup your hands in front of you. When I count to three you will take the cigarette and lock it in between your hands. It will change color. Close your hands when I say 'Go.'"*

Hold the borrowed cigarette near the bottom with the

tips of your right thumb and forefinger. Bring your right
hand up alongside your head at about ear level, then bring it
down again toward the cupped hands as you count *"One."*
Bring your hand back again and count *"Two"* as you come
down. On the third movement, bring your hand up but leave
the cigarette tucked behind your ear (Figure 98). The hand
comes down as before as you count. *"Three. Go!"*

Figure 98

The spectator grabs at the cigarette, and you show your
empty hand. He has no cigarette. *"Something went wrong.
The cigarette is gone, and you are turning color."*

Take his hands and cup them again. Strike them with
your index finger. *"That's four."* Reach up and get the
cigarette, bringing it down into his hand at *"Five."* Do
another cigarette trick to follow this.

RISING UP

This is a good opener for a series of cigarette tricks. You will have to prepare it a moment or two in advance. Remove a single cigarette from your package, and tuck it at the back of the package between the cellophane and the pack.

When ready to do the trick, take the pack from your pocket carefully so as not to expose the back. The cigarettes are held as in Figure 99, with your thumb under the single cigarette and your fingers on either side of the pack. The audience sees only the front.

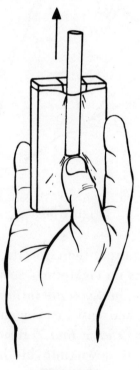

Figure 99

"Try my cigarettes, they're very unusual." Push the cigarette up with your thumb through the cellophane. It will apparently rise from the center of the package. Your left hand takes it as it comes up to the top. *"These cigarettes use light tobacco—that's why they can float. And they also have another strange feature."*

Take the cigarette in the right hand and roll it as you turn your wrist doing the paddle move we described earlier. *"There is no name on this one."* The cigarette appears to be blank.

A DOZEN FOOLERS

Knotting a Cigarette You can bet that you can tie a knot in a cigarette without damaging it. Here's how: remove the cellophane from your cigarette package. Flatten a section of it and roll your cigarette in the paper. You will form a long tube which can then be knotted without damage to the cigarette.

Huff and Puff *"Smoking is bad for my health, so whenever I get a cigarette, I let it smoke by itself. I'll show you how."* Clasp your hands together, thumbs crossed on top. Place the unlighted end of the cigarette in the small hole formed at the bases of the two thumbs. By squeezing your hands together and relaxing them, the cigarette appears to puff by itself (Figure 100).

Not So Hot This one was a favorite of the late Shelly Deifik. If your fingers have been chilled by being in contact with an ice cube or any very cold surface, you can hold the burning tip of a cigarette between the index finger and

Figure 100

thumb for a moment without getting burned. Then take a puff and hand it to someone else. *"Care to try it?"*

Rings of Smoke   You can get beautiful smoke rings this way. Pull the cellophane wrapper halfway off the package of cigarettes. Touch the tip of your burning cigarette to the cellophane long enough to get a small hole. Take a puff and blow the smoke into the hole. Now tap the edge of the cellophane lightly (X), and you will get a series of perfect rings (Figure 101).

A Little Balance   One cigarette will appear to be perfectly balanced on the end of another, with both of them held vertically. The secret is to break a tiny piece off the end of a toothpick. Insert this in the top cigarette before you pretend to balance them. Your fingers should hide the toothpick as you stick it into the top of the second cigarette.

Save Your Lungs   *"The Surgeon General claims that smoking is hazardous to your health. That's because the smoke gets into your lungs. Here is how to prevent it."* Pretend to inhale by raising your chest as you blow gently through the cigarette. It will look as though you were taking a puff. The end of the cigarette will even glow. Remove the cigarette from your lips and blow out very hard. Naturally, no smoke comes out.

A Lighter Gag   For people who like to bum cigarettes, this gag is fun—but dangerous. *"I'll bet I can make your package a cigarette lighter."* Remove a single cigarette. *"There. It is now one cigarette lighter."* The danger comes from telling this joke.

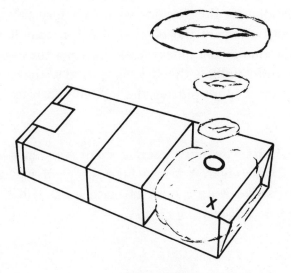

Figure 101

Another Gag   Inhale a deep puff of smoke secretly. Now bring your cigarette in front of your face with a flourish, so that you get everyone's attention. Place the unlighted end in your ear, tip your head, and blow smoke from your mouth. It's a funny sight.

Jumping Cigar Band   Remove the band from a cigar and put it on the middle finger of your right hand. Strike only the middle and ring fingers against the open left palm. Do this twice. On the third try, bring your index finger up and strike the palm with only the index and middle fingers. The band appears to jump from one finger to another (Figures 102 and 103).

Both Sides Lit   This stunt is best done with a cigar. The lighted cigar is between your lips. Bring your right hand up to take the cigar between the index and middle fingers, with the backs of your fingers touching your mouth. Your palm faces the audience. Rotate your wrist in a forward motion, pushing the bottom of the cigar upward so that it is held between the thumb and index finger. Now put the cigar back in your mouth, pulling the thumb toward your face. The illusion is that you are putting the lighted end back in your mouth.

Quick Light   Secretly insert a small wooden match in the end of your cigar. You can take the cigar out of your pocket and strike it on a book of matches: it will light. *"I love these new self-starting cigars."*

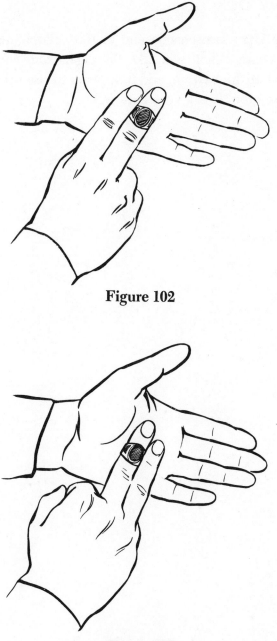

Figure 102

Figure 103

Rising Up   Loosen one end of the cellophane wrapper on your cigar. When you take the cigar from your pocket, squeeze it at the bottom, and it appears to rise up out of the top of the tube. It is a very cute sight.

Pot-pourri

SUSPENSION

By this time you are probably convinced that most magic is done under the table in your lap. It's true that at dinner this is the only place to prepare your tricks without leaving the room, so here we go again.

Tear a small piece of cellophane from a package of cigarettes. Try to tear it in a circle a little larger than a nickel, so that it will make an invisible top for a soda bottle. The disc is kept in your right hand at the first joint of your middle and ring fingers. If you wet the fingers a bit it will adhere to your hand until you are ready.

Lift a small, half-filled bottle of soda or water. Set the bottle in your left palm and cover the top with your right fingers. You are secretly adding the small disc as your right hand comes over the bottle. This should seal the opening. The bottle is now held between both hands.

"This is an upside-down trick. If I turn the bottle upside down, the liquid does not spill." Do this by turning both hands upside down. *"Of course, my hand is in the way. But if I take my hand away we have what we magicians call a 'suspension.'"* Remove the right hand and the liquid remains. The cellophane is practically invisible at this point. A sharp rap on the bottom of the bottle, over an empty glass, will release the liquid and at the same time get rid of the cellophane.

Now that you have an empty bottle, bet that it can be

lifted by a single straw. To do this, bend the straw and set it in the bottle. As the straw goes back to its original shape it wedges in the bottle and you can lift it (Figure 104).

ANOTHER BEER?

This is a bottle betcha that will earn you another beer or soda. Turn your empty beer or soda bottle upside down on top of a dollar bill. Bet another drink that you can remove the bill without lifting the bottle. To win the bet, merely roll the bill toward the bottle tightly. A pencil will help if you have one. The bill moves toward you and the bottle will remain in place (Figure 105). Try it.

CANDLE MAGIC

Dinner by candlelight is romantic, and you can also use the candle for some good tricks. In the matchbook section of this book there is a stunt where you hold the match in front of a glass and blow it out through the center. You can do this with a candle held in front of a soda bottle.

Here is another startling effect. Secretly push the edge of a dime a little way into the side of the candle near you. Do this by making a little slit in the soft wax. No one can see the coin if it faces you. Show both hands empty. Roll your fingers around the candle, moving up toward the top, and produce the dime from the flame.

Light a match from the candle. Blow out the candle and hold the match several inches above the flame. The flame will magically travel down the smoke and relight the candle. It's a pretty effect.

Figure 104

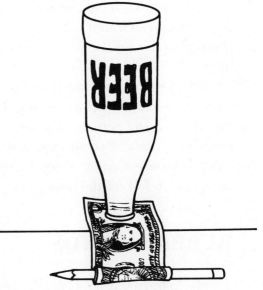

Figure 105

If you have two candles, place them in your spectator's hands, between the knuckles of his middle fingers. Now light them and tell the spectator, *"Please think of a number; then blow out the candles."* When he blows the candles out, sing "Happy Birthday" to him. If you arrange for the others at the table to join in, you can have a good laugh.

DRINKING STRAWS

You can do other things with straws, besides lifting a bottle. You can cause the straw to roll with "static electricity," as you did with a cigarette earlier. And if you remove the paper from a packaged straw, pulling it off accordion style, you can do the worm trick. Here's how:

Tear off the top of the straw wrapper. Push the paper down along the straw so that you have a small crumpled piece in your left hand. Set it on the table. *"This is Oscar, my pet worm. Watch him when I give him a drink."* Put a few drops of water on the paper and it will wriggle as if it were alive.

If you balance a straw over the edge of the table you can cause it to follow your magic wand (pen) quite mysteriously. Secretly rub the pen on your sleeve or woolen suit to create static electricity. Pass the pen under the straw and make it move from side to side. A rapid downward motion will cause the straw to fall off the table.

RUBBER BANDS

My old friend and magic teacher, Abe Hurwitz, is writing an entire book about magic with rubber bands. Here are just two of the hundreds of tricks you can do with them.

Elmer   Hook a rubber band around your left pinky. Pull it up across your palm so that it stretches as far as it will go. Lock the loop in place by pushing it with your thumb against the side of your left index finger. The palm is held flat, facing you, with the loose loop of the rubber band showing over it. *"This is my rubber-band worm. His name is Elmer. Elmer, it's time to go downstairs for lunch."* The slightest relaxation of your left thumb will cause the rubber band to creep in a wormlike fashion down into the left palm. It looks very much alive and is a great favorite with children. They actually talk to it if you present it properly.

Snap and Jump   Place a rubber band around the index and middle fingers of your left hand, at the base of the fingers (Figure 106). Close your left hand as your right hand pulls the rubber band down, stretching it so that the tips of all four fingers are inside (Figure 107). The hand is held in a fistlike position with the palm facing the floor. Snap the fingers of your right hand over the rubber band. At the same time, open the left. The rubber band jumps from the first two to the last two fingers. Reverse the procedure and watch it jump back (Figure 108).

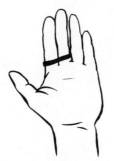

Figure 106   **Figure 107**   **Figure 108**

LINKING PAPER CLIPS

Put a few paper clips in your pocket, or ask the restaurant cashier for some. This one is a goodie.

"One of the oldest tricks in magic is one called the Linking Ring trick. It has been done for centuries and is still performed today. Solid rings pass through other solid rings, defying the laws of science. I would do it for you, but I don't believe in breaking laws. However, with these paper clips I'll show you something very similar."

Fold a dollar bill in thirds as in Figure 109. Place one clip around the first and second folds. Place the other clip around the second and third folds. If you pull the upper corners away from you in a quick motion, the paper clips will link and drop to the table. Practice this at home until you get the knack.

Figure 109

MY CARD

If you're having a business lunch, the best way to sneak in some selling would be with magic. Here is a nice stunt you can do with your business card. Take the card from your pocket and place it in your left hand, holding it by the shorter edges between the thumb and middle fingers.

"This is my business card. I want to show you how strong it is." Your right hand takes the card by the longer edges (Figure 110).

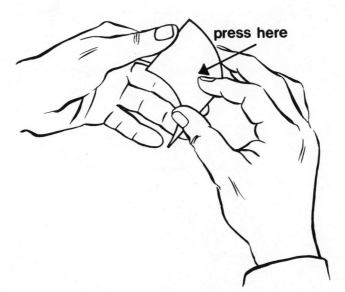

press here

Figure 110

Your right thumb on one side, middle finger on the other. Squeeze the card as you press the right index finger into the middle (Figure 111).

The card will fold down into a pincer-like shape. Place this over a salt shaker and squeeze, and the card will lift the weight (Figure 112).

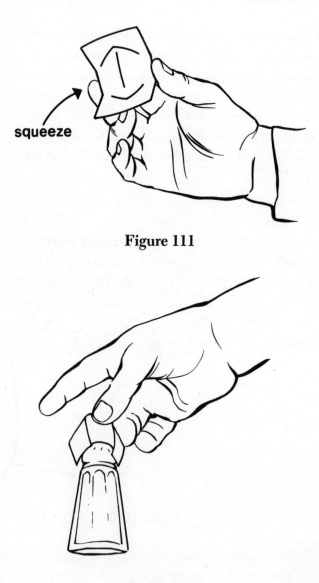

squeeze

Figure 111

Figure 112

"Take this with you." Hand the spectator your card. *"Use it to pick up your telephone when you want to call me. I hope it will be soon."*

As a ventriloquist I find this a very cute stunt, especially for children. I paint a set of lips on each edge of the card with a marking pen. By squeezing it gently the mouth opens and closes, and I have an impromptu puppet.

COMES THE CHECK

Our magic dinner is over, and in a restaurant each meal ends with the dinner check. Here is one last trick for the road. You can use it as a betcha stunt to see who pays the tab.

Hold the check by the top with your right index finger and thumb. Your left hand is positioned under the bill, thumb on one side, index finger on the other (Figure 113).

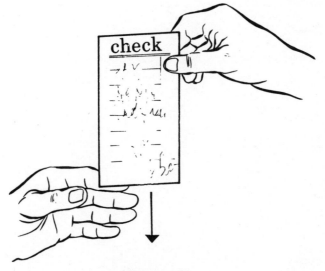

Figure 113

The fingers are held about a half inch apart on each side of the check. Count *"One, two, three, go!"* Drop the bill from your right hand and easily catch it in your left as it falls.

Now comes the fun. Challenge the spectator to catch it as you drop it. If he can, you pay the check. If he misses, he pays.

He positions his fingers as you did earlier, and you count. *"One, two, three, go!"* Drop the bill a split second before you say *"Go."* His brain cannot send the signal to his fingertips fast enough to catch it. And if you need the money try it again, double or nothing.

4

Let Us Entertain Them

In the preceding pages you have found many tricks that I hope you will use to amuse and amaze your friends. You learned the how of doing the tricks. You have seen why they work. I have given you guidelines on how to instruct your spectators and how to create interest in the action. But doing a trick is not enough. You must use the trick in conjunction with your own personality to make the whole effect entertaining.

How does one entertain? First of all, your own personality must always come through. Never try to be someone else. If you put on mannerisms or gestures that are not natural, you will soon be found out, and your magic is no longer fun. Be yourself.

Patter, the words you speak, must also come naturally. Unless certain phrases are part of the routine, let the words be your own. I have supplied patter here as a guide to your performance. In most cases it should be changed to fit your own creative presentation. Make up your own stories for each trick. The few times you must stick to the script are indicated in this book—when you must give the spectator *specific* instructions. Reread a few of the tricks and see how you can change the patter. Try not to make your speech sound memorized. Ad lib a little; it can be more fun than you realize.

Take over. Don't be afraid to take command of your audience. Do your trick and handle it your way. People are always willing to follow a good leader. Give your directions with authority, but remember that politeness is a must for any entertainer. Saying "please" is a simple but effective way to get action from even a suspicious spectator.

Study every detail of your trick so that it will look perfect. Never suggest that "this may not work," unless you are trying for a comic effect. Practice those things that are a bit more difficult. Hesitation during a performance will take away your credibility, so make sure that you know every move before you begin.

Keep your tricks simple. If there are too many explanations or extra movements, you will complicate the magic and bore the spectator. I have taken all the sleight of hand away so your job is much easier.

Never repeat a trick or use a similar trick in the same performance. Magic relies on the surprise of what is going to happen. The audience must never know this in advance. The only time a trick may be repeated is when the repetition is designed for a specific effect. I have indicated where you can repeat an effect.

Watch your angles. If you feel that you might get caught by someone sitting too close, stop and think before you act. If you do not think the angle of vision is right for the trick, either change your position or *do not do the trick.* Unless you are a great comedy performer, a trick that fails will spoil the magic.

Routining your act is very important. Your presentation should be well balanced, offering a variety of effects instead of the same type of trick each time. Too many vanishes or too many productions can be boring. Too many salt tricks or an overload of number tricks will also put people to sleep. Don't burden your audience—leave everyone wanting more. Start with some of your best material in each category. Do a few tricks and build up to your very best trick for a closing. Saving the blockbuster for the end will leave your audience with a lasting impression of your talents. Above all, don't perform too long. Nothing is worse than a boring magician.

Don't show off with magic. Your reputation will precede you, so you needn't thrust yourself on the spectator who doesn't care to see a trick. Be ready to perform at the drop of a spoon, but don't push. If your audience does not know that you are a magician, they will find out soon enough when you casually do something startling. A good trick will get the conversation going. Never, never, never start off with, *"Hey, you gotta see this trick, and this one, and this one . . . "*

Learn something about magic. A respect for your art will enhance your performance. Read a few good books on the history of magic. Learn about the magicians of the past and present, and you will develop a satisfying kinship with them. Knowing about the basics of magic is like learning the notes on the piano. For example, you should know that there are eight basic effects created by the magician. (An effect is what the spectator thinks he is seeing.) Here are the eight basics:

1. *The Vanish.* Causing an object to disappear from sight or seem invisible.

2. *The Production.* Making an object appear from apparently nowhere.

3. *A Transformation.* Causing one object to change into another.

4. *A Transposition.* Causing two objects to change places with one another.

5. *A Penetration.* Causing one solid object to pass through another.

6. *A Restoration.* Making whole an object that has previously been destroyed.

7. *The Levitation.* Making objects rise and float in the air without visible means of support.

8. *A Suspension.* Making a person or object hang in the air by a single support, defying scientific laws of balance.

There are subdivisions such as the Escape Trick, which is a form of penetration in which a person or thing securely bound in one place becomes free. Mentalism, while using some of the above effects, is a completely separate form of magic.

Secrecy must be preserved. The attractiveness of magic is due largely to the fact that there is an air of mystery around it. People cannot understand how it is done. The real secret of magic is in the presentation and misdirection. Once someone learns the secret working of the trick it ceases to become magic. You are then a person who does "tricks" rather than one who performs magic. It is very hard to keep the secret of a magic trick—especially for the beginner, who is proud of his success. Remind yourself that if the secret were known there would be no success.

Keeping the secret of your own trick is not enough. The first rule of magic is that you must respect the secrets of *all* tricks and all magicians. You might see another magician doing a trick that you recognize. Keep quiet! Never expose him or his trick. You might want to meet with him privately to discuss your mutual interests, but never embarrass him with "Oh, I do that one" or "I know how you did that" or worse, explaining what he did in front of another spectator.

The last word on secrecy is *practice*. The worst exposer of magic is a poor magician. The tricks in this book do not require a great deal of preparation, but proficiency is always helped by practice.

Misdirection. This word is the key to magic. The hand is really not quicker than the eye. The eye is just not looking in the right place. Misdirection is the art of diverting the eye and the mind of the spectator. Looking back on the tricks you just read, you will note that in many places I have tried to give you some indication of when and how to misdirect. Here are some more important pointers.

Your *eyes* play a very important role in misdirection. You will find that if your eyes are looking in a particular direction, the spectator's eyes will follow them. If a coin is supposed to be in your left hand, you must look at your left hand. You will look at that hand even if the coin is secretly falling into your lap. You won't look into your lap because the spectator will alway follow your eyes. Think back to the Vanishing Salt Shaker trick. You have conditioned the spectator to keep his eye on the coin. You watch the coin as the shaker disappears quietly.

This brings us to *conditioning,* the technique of getting the spectator to accept your moves as natural. In the trick we just used as an example, every time you moved the coin forward with the left hand, your right hand brought the shaker back to the edge of the table. Your spectator was conditioned to seeing the shaker taken away from his focal point. When you did your secret move, he was not looking at the movement. It was natural to him.

Physical action can also be used for misdirection. For example, if the left hand is brought toward the spectator for a "blow" to help the vanish, he cannot look anywhere but at the hand. He must perform a physical action.

Your *patter* is essential to misdirection. *"Keep your eye on the coin."* His brain accepts the fact that a coin is where you said it was, and his eye is on the coin that isn't there anymore.

Look back over some of the tricks you found most enjoyable, and this time find the points of misdirection in each. It is fun to perform magic, but almost as much fun to analyze it for your own edification.

The magic you have just learned is called *close-up magic*, because it can be done literally under the nose of your spectator. But you are not confined to the dinner table. You can expand into larger areas such as meeting halls or night-clubs and perform what is called *club* or *parlor magic*. For larger groups you will need to make your magic props a bit more visible. Your mind-reading effects will suit nicely here. If you decide to go further into magic, you can find many good books on the subject of using larger props.

You may even decide to do *stage magic*, which requires large props and illusions that can be seen by a theater-sized audience. Your mental tricks will then require a large blackboard instead of a paper pad. But you are already on the road to bigger things, and I hope you will keep going.

Find an area of magic you like best and specialize. Add some poise, friendliness, comedy, mystery, self-ridicule, charm, and self-confidence to your routine. Sell yourself first and your tricks second. That's entertainment.

Bibliography

Anderson, George B. *Magic Digest.* Chicago, Follett, 1972.

Christopher, Milbourne. *Illustrated History of Magic.* New York, Crowell, 1973.

Dexter, Will. *131 Magic Tricks for Amateurs.* New York, Arco, 1958.

Garcia, Frank, and Schindler, George. *Amedeo's Continental Magic.* New York, Million Dollar Productions, 1974.

Gardner, Martin. *Mathematics, Magic and Mystery.* New York, Dover, 1956.

Gibson, Walter. *Professional Magic for Amateurs.* New York, Dover, 1974.

Hugard's Magic Monthly (magicians' periodical). Various issues.

Kaye, Marvin. *The Stein and Day Handbook of Magic.* New York, Stein and Day, 1973.

Phoenix Magazine (magicians' periodical). Various issues.

Randi, James. *The Magic of Uri Geller.* New York, Ballantine, 1975.

Thurston, Howard. *300 Tricks You Can Do.* Sandpiper Press, 1927.

Willmarth, Philip R. *Fun with a Handkerchief.* Chicago, Magic, Inc., 1969.

Index